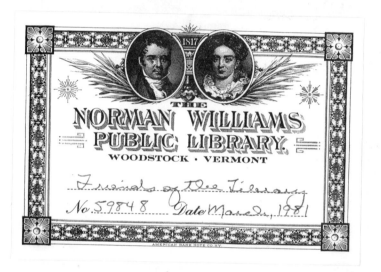

A New Look at
CROCHET

A New Look at CROCHET

Using Basic Stitches to Create Modern Designs

by Elyse Sommer and Mike Sommer

CROWN PUBLISHERS, INC.
NEW YORK

Printed in the United States of America
Published simultaneously in Canada by General Publishing Company Limited

Design by Nedda Balter

Library of Congress Cataloging in Publication Data
Sommer, Elyse and Mike
  A new look at crochet: using basic stitches to create modern designs
  Bibliography: p.
  1. Crocheting. I. Title.
TT820.S62 1975   746.4'34   74-30265
ISBN 0-517-51607-1
ISBN 0-517-51608-X pbk.

Contents

Foreword

The idea for A NEW LOOK AT CROCHET was born out of a growing belief that crochet is much more than a pleasant and useful pastime. As we got deeper into the book—photographing outstanding work and interviewing crochet artists and museum curators who have exhibited crochet as a part of the off-loom scene—this belief was affirmed again and again.

We hope that the ideas and methods illustrated will stimulate anyone interested in art and design to pick up a crochet hook and yarn (a roll of string will do to start) and give free rein to her creative instincts. Few crafts are as easy to learn, requiring such simple, readily accessible, and portable tools and supplies. Outstanding results can be achieved in a short time.

Though crochet has behind it a long history and tradition, its use as a medium of self-expression and originality is relatively new. Chapters 3, 4, 5, and 6 give specific instructions for mastering basic stitch skills. There are books with illustrations and instructions for hundreds of other stitches and patterns, but we have purposely limited the number of stitches taught to the most basic and useful ones since we feel a mastery of an extensive stitch vocabulary is second-ary to developing a sense for the color, form, and design potentially inherent in crochet.

The stitch and technique demonstrations are arranged in logical progres-sion, with suggestions for and illustrations of starting projects following im-mediately. This will enable the novice crocheter to enjoy the satisfaction of ap-plying his new skills without delay to a completely original design.

Much of the illustrated work was photographed in its developmental stages so that the reader will have a clear understanding of the construction con-cepts involved and thus apply them to his own designs. These demonstrations range from useful items such as clocks, clothing, and pillows, to hangings and sculpture. Unlike stitch-by-stitch instructions that call for mechanical repro-duction of complicated-sounding and often confusing symbols and abbrevia-tions, the step-by-step photos are intended to guide and inspire. Ideally, they will serve as springboards for the reader's own ideas. With crochet more in vogue than ever before, many attractive crochet items complete with stitch-by-stitch patterns are published in magazines and by yarn and pattern com-panies. Readers who want to make some of these designs for themselves will find they have a better understanding of the directions given, once they have worked with this book. Best of all they will have the conceptual knowledge to make alterations and adjustments to suit their own taste. Thus even stitch-by-stitch patterns can become completely individualized.

This book presents just a sprinkling of the truly astounding variety of things that can be crocheted. As you study the work of others, your own imag-ination will take over. By referring to the stitch and technique instructions in the early chapters and studying how other artists handled their particular problems, you will be able to work out your own.

Whatever your tastes, talents, or fantasies, crochet is an all-absorbing medium for expressing them. It is truly a something-for-everyone art and craft. So get out your hook, some yarn, and welcome to the wonderful world of crochet.

Acknowledgments

Tops on our acknowledgment list are, of course, all the talented crocheters who shared their work and their thoughts with us. They are truly our coauthors. Our thanks also to the many people at various galleries and museums who helped us obtain photographs and put us in touch with artists in their areas: Doris Bowman of the Smithsonian Institution; Elizabeth Finkbeiner of the Portland Art Museum; Maureen Herbert of the Museum of Contemporary Crafts; Mary Stephens Nelson of The Boise Gallery of Art. No book of this sort would be possible without good library resources. We particularly appreciated the facilities of the American Crafts Council Library, the New York Public Library, and the help of Robert Thomason of the Hewlett-Woodmere Library. The prompt and capable processing of our prints by Alan and Ben Ageman greatly facilitated our task. Last but not least, thank you, Brandt Aymar, for lending your always excellent editorial hand while giving us free rein over the content and layout of the book.

All illustrated work unless otherwise identified by Elyse Sommer.

All photographs unless otherwise identified by Mike Sommer.

Elyse and Mike Sommer, Woodmere, Long Island, New York
1974

Baroque Coat. Dina Schwartz.

Crochet Then and Now

1

In our interviews with contributing artists one idea was expressed again and again: "My involvement with crochet is different from the old-fashioned doily approach." And so is the whole concept of crochet today. That is why we have titled our book A NEW LOOK AT CROCHET.

When crochet first joined the ranks of popular needlecrafts, the crocheters of the day did indeed turn our thousands of doilies, along with collars, tablecloths, bedspreads, and the like. All these items were beautifully crafted in fine cotton, usually all white. The emphasis was on intricacy of workmanship and meticulous copying of patterns. The anti-doily revolution is really not a revolt against the fine craftsmanship that typified the doily look but against the quality of sameness and the emphasis on imitation rather than innovation. No matter how experimental some of today's crochet may be, it is nevertheless grounded in traditional stitches. The newness is in the use to which the stitches are put, the yarns that are used, and the statements that are made. In order to appreciate the new look that is making crochet one of the most exciting new-old mediums for both artists and hobbyists, let's go back not just to the "doily era" but to its very beginning.

History of Crochet

As with many of the needlecrafts, the history of crochet is often more a matter of conjecture than fact. The very perishability of fibers as opposed to metals and pottery has provided historians with little actual data to study. However, some of the ancient tombs of Egypt did yield some garments with frayed edges suggestive of some type of primitive lace. Since lace and crochet are closely identified, it is not too farfetched to assume that these ancient garments are evidence of an early form of crochet lace produced by bits of cotton being twisted around primitive man's fingers.

Woolen garments dating back to the Bronze Age have also been found. But again, there are very few samples that are not so deteriorated that historians could ever really study these fragments in terms of construction techniques. Some did specify that these were "nonwoven" garments. Ecclesiastic historians cited tunics and loincloths among their findings, but again, not being craftsmen, made little effort to identify the techniques used to make the apparel worn by biblical characters. Clothing was either woven or "wrought," which might have meant crocheted, but could also mean wrought by means of netting, looping, braiding, twisting, or knitting. Heinz Edgar Kiewe, in a fascinating and scholarly book entitled *The Sacred History of Knitting,* traced knitting needles and crochet hooks back to the time of Christ. He concluded that crochet hooks were probably everyday implements of that time and refers to the story of one of the followers of Jesus, Akida ben Joseph (50–137), who was said to have used a crochet hook that he might spend his time as a shepherd more usefully. The author, in commenting on the story of the Exodus from Egypt, speculates that the slaves probably knitted garments after plucking wool off the camels and sheep in response to the Lord's command to cover themselves. Since the garments had to be loose and cool in that hot climate and the slaves probably had to make the cloth as they marched along, we picture finger crochet an even more likely method.

On the European continent the association between knitting, crochet, and lace is so closely interwoven as to be almost inseparable. Fine lace was much valued and from the thirteenth to the sixteenth century lacemaking was nuns' work as much as illuminating manuscripts was considered monks' work. More is written about the nuns' point lace and bobbin lacework than their use of the crochet hook, although it was apparently in use by the sixteenth or seventeenth century. Crochet seemed to be classed as something of a poor cousin to other lacework. French nuns were the first to use the crochet hook; hence the name crochet is a derivation of the French word *croche* or *croc.*

It was in Ireland, during the famine of the 1840s, that crochet proved its real worth, and it is no exaggeration to say that the crochet hook saved thousands of Irish people from starvation. The credit for teaching people to help themselves by means of crocheting goes not only to the nuns who knew and taught the craft but to an enterprising lady, a Mrs. W. C. Roberts of County Kildare, who used to teach the poor to knit. When she found orders for knitwear failing just at a time when the need for earnings was greatest, Mrs. Roberts decided to experiment by switching to crochet. The experiment was a great success and Mrs. Roberts's method of spreading knowledge of the craft was further proof of her initiative. Everyone taught by her was required to teach thirty others. Thus Irish crochet became an article of commercial importance, a status it maintained even after the famine.

Crochet as a Hobby

After the Irish famine crochet assumed new importance, this time not as a lifesaver but as a leisure-time delight. The steady rise of its popularity ever since makes one wonder why it took so long for ladies of leisure to discover its charms.

The Irish who migrated to the United States brought along their crochet skills. However, according to Mrs. Ann S. Stephens in her book, *The Ladies' Complete Guide to Crochet, Fancy Knitting and Needlework,* published in 1854, "while in England and Ireland crochet work has risen to the dignity of an art, in this country, crochet work can only be denominated an accomplishment." A firm moralist as well as needlework historian, Mrs. Stephens cautioned against considering crochet as merely an elegant way of "wileing" away time, but urged her readers instead to recognize it as "one of those gentle means by which women are kept feminine and ladylike in this fast age." Morality notwithstanding, the lady was not above a bit of feminine trickery. "What excuse should we have for casting down our eyes when other people's eyes become troublesome?" she chattily confides. "Every lady knows how many heart tremors can be carried off in a vigorous twist of the crochet-needle." Dear Abby couldn't have advised better!

By 1863 crochet was so popular that numerous patterns were published and special cottons were manufactured for crocheting. Though crochet work was done with a variety of yarns and ribbons, cotton was the predominant material used. Filet crochet was the most popular type of crochet and this was always in all-white cotton, probably because of the symbolic associations with purity and holiness. The most popular designs also carried religious significance: grapes, stars, etc., all associated with religious symbolism and very suitable as motifs for doilies, bedspreads, and similar projects.

Women's magazines such as *The Ladies' World, Godey's Lady's Book and Magazine, New Idea Woman's Magazine,* to name just a few, regularly carried patterns for crochet work. Most of the patterns were for filet crochet. A very popular magazine of the early twentieth century, *The Modern Priscilla* sometimes carried three separate crochet instruction pages in one issue. Some of these pages reflected an earnest effort on the part of the editors to find new uses for the crochet work, giving instructions for small crocheted bowls as well as the usual flat pieces, and covered mirror frames. Sometimes the editors even attempted to get away from the all-cotton filet lace approach by suggesting the use of completely different materials. One 1915 issue carried instructions for a hat to be made with raffia twine, truly a forerunner of today's innovative use of all types of materials.

Contests were another aspect of the crochet scene which undoubtedly helped to foster its popularity. In the 1920s there was a Priscilla Crochet Con-

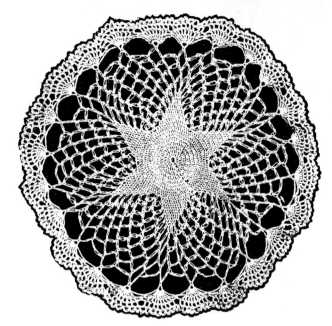

Crochet doily with star center, from *New Idea Woman's Magazine*, 1905.

Crochet Square for Antimacassar, which originally appeared in *Godey's Lady's Book and Magazine*.

test with 80 cash prizes for the clever wielder of crochet hooks. In 1937 the Nation-wide Crochet Contest, which became a big annual event up to the 1940s, was sponsored by the leading American manufacturers of crochet cottons. The emphasis was obviously on entries made with cotton, although categories covered a wide range of items from household to fashion accessories. Entry designs reflected the interests and issues of the day. For example, the 1939 contest drew eight American flags complete with crocheted tassels, a pillow cover portraying the meeting of President Roosevelt and King George VI, and a crocheted airplane! In addition to contests for excellence in workmanship and design by cotton crocheters, there were contests such as the Crochet Speed contests, with the title of Lady Nimble Fingers going to the lady who crocheted the longest edging in a one-hour run. These events were so popular that they were covered on radio by well-known celebrities of the day.

It was the widespread popularity of filet crochet that led to the use of thousands of doilies and antimacassars for decorating chairbacks, tabletops, and dressers in what seemed to be almost every home throughout the country. As wool, and eventually synthetics, came more into use a somewhat more sophisticated crochet look followed. With the boom in nostalgia in general and Art Deco in particular, some publishers are today reprinting patterns for crocheted hats and sweaters of the thirties. The newer look in crochet is also being reflected in the new patterns appearing in booklets issued by yarn manufacturers and pattern companies and in current magazines.

Doilies and antimacassars made by Elyse Sommer's grandmother who was a true craftswoman. In addition to meticulously executing the popular designs of her day, she invented many of her own patterns for both knitting and crochet, though unfortunately no samples of these were to be found.

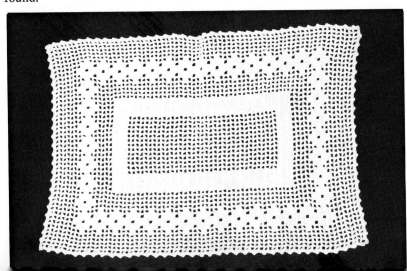

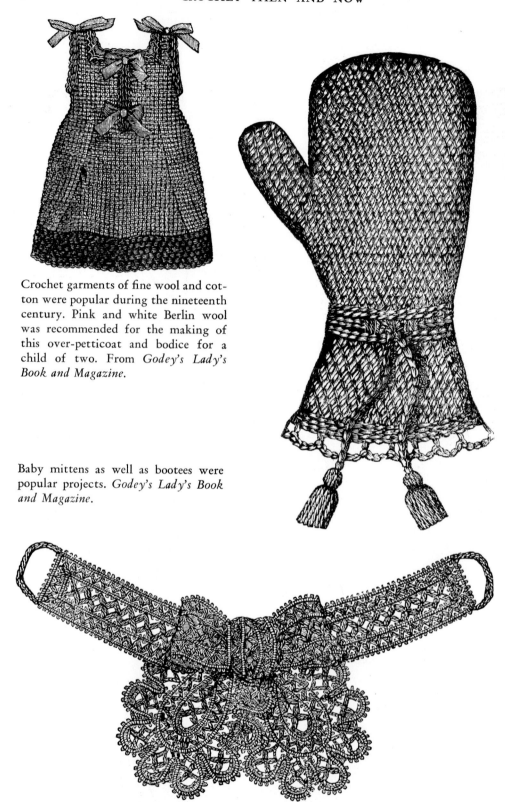

Crochet garments of fine wool and cotton were popular during the nineteenth century. Pink and white Berlin wool was recommended for the making of this over-petticoat and bodice for a child of two. From *Godey's Lady's Book and Magazine.*

Baby mittens as well as bootees were popular projects. *Godey's Lady's Book and Magazine.*

A curtain band from *Godey's Lady's Book and Magazine.*

Filet Crochet Gifts

Filet crochet gift items from *The Ladies' World*, 1915. The little dishes might be considered forerunners of some of the pottery shown in Chapter 12.

Camisole tops of Irish crochet were very fashionable. Photo courtesy Smithsonian Institution.

Collars have always been stylish accessories. This Irish crochet collar with shamrock, grape, and flower motifs is in the collection of the Smithsonian Institution. Photo courtesy of the Smithsonian Institution.

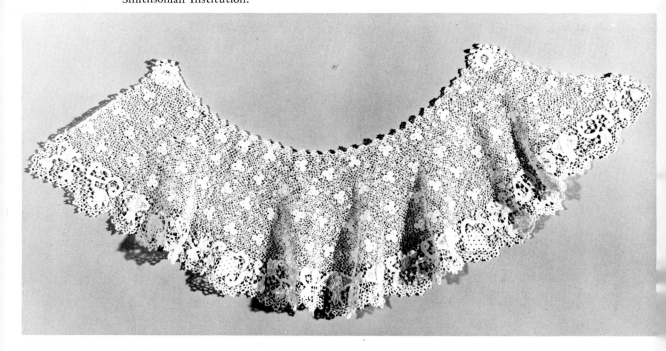

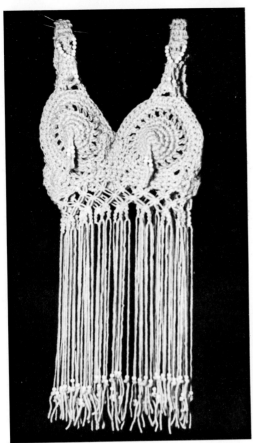

Though few people would either make or wear camisoles these days, the past always offers inspiration to the modern artist, to wit, this hanging titled BAN THE BRA by Bucky King. Wool and beads are used.

Mary Lou Higgins adds a crocheted collar to a handwoven dress. The collar is reminiscent of the Irish crochet cape collars. The overall effect, however, is distinctly contemporary. Photo by Edward Higgins.

The editors of *The Modern Priscilla* often suggested new uses for filet crochet, for example, these frames from a 1922 edition.

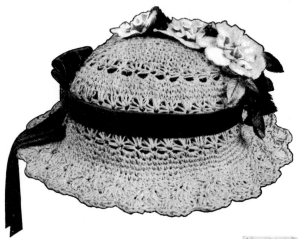

Though the use of cords and twine as part of crochet work is considered a part of the new look in crochet, nothing is *really* completely new. This hat of raffia twine was featured as a how-to item in *The Modern Priscilla*, June 1915.

Detail view of a bedspread, circa 1930. Collection of Rhoda Schiffreen.

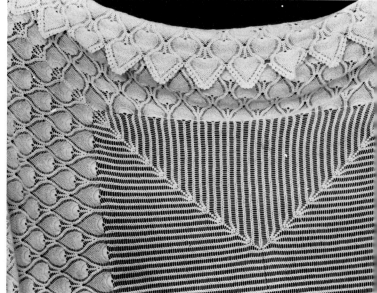

Hats in jute, straw, and ribbon by a contemporary designer, Alison Schiff.

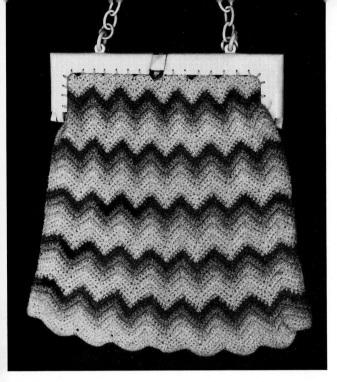

Cara Sherman, an Art Deco collector, proudly uses this pale blue, beige, and green ripple stitch bag. The stitches are worked into the holes of the bone handle, a technique much in use today, especially when combining crochet and leather (Chapter 10).

Crochet's Emergence as an Art Form

The true blossoming of crochet as art as well as popular hobby is a fairly recent development. It was during the 1960s that artists interested in textiles and fibers began serious experimentation with crochet, responding to the greater freedom of working in any direction and shape, with many colors and textures. The International Wall Hangings Show at the Museum of Modern Art in 1968, which included crochet, became an inspirational springboard for many. Fiber shows throughout the world have given the medium a more prominent place each year. A show on body coverings at the Portland Museum of Art, the Baroque show, and a clothing show at the Museum of Contemporary Crafts, a fun and fantasy show traveling throughout the country under the sponsorship of the Xerox Corporation, are just some notable exhibits that include fine examples of crochet work. Prizes in mixed media shows are frequently being taken by crocheters, and all-crochet shows are no longer just a dream.

Crocheters Then and Now

Who are the people who crochet?

To be sure, *The Ladies' Complete Guide to Crochet, Fancy Knitting and Needlework* and *The Modern Priscilla* addressed themselves to genteel ladies. Today's crocheters, however, can no more be stereotyped than today's crochet work. More and more men are seeking creative self-fulfillment with so-called gentler pursuits, something we see as a hopeful sign in an otherwise much troubled world. Actually men have always been part, if not an integral one, of the crochet scene. If shepherds in ancient times crocheted, then the first crocheters were indeed men. When crochet was taught as a means of self-support in Ireland, boys and men were happy to learn, and did. Even when crochet became mostly a popular pastime, men did not completely step out of the picture. The Nation-wide contests always had a For Men Only division, which never lacked entries. Prizewinners included a ranch hand from California, a metal polisher from Ohio, and a railroad man from New York. Their work was no different from the women's in terms of stitches, yarns, and projects. Again, when the time came to break with tradition, a man's name, Walter Nottingham, was right in the forefront.

Today men, women, and children—artists, teachers, and hobbyists—are crocheting more than ever, exploring more and newer methods each day. Their crochet work has outgrown the old parlor worktable and is now being done when traveling in cars, buses, and on planes. It is its history and tradition, its enormous potential for a future combining the best of past and present, that makes crochet a vital and valuable art and craft.

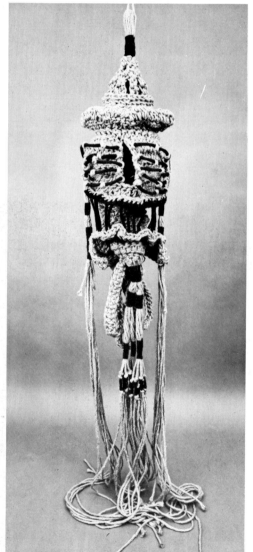

Experimental sculpture by a talented young male crocheter, Jeff Berman. Photo courtesy artist.

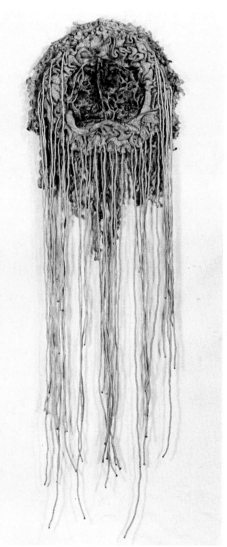

FUSES. Crocheted hanging by one of the innovators in sculptural crochet, Walter Nottingham. Photo courtesy artist.

Delia Brock and Lorraine Bodger typify many of today's adventurous young crocheters. Working without patterns, with mostly single and double crochets, they have designed and sold crochet clothes to leading shops and boutiques. Photo by Lowell Bodger.

Mary Lou Higgins. Photo by Ed Higgins.

Jane Knight. Photo by Dick Knight.

Two Midwestern crocheters, Mary Lou Higgins and Jane Knight, have contributed enormously to contemporary crochet.

Sculptural forms created by Jane Knight. Photo by Dick Knight.

Dina Schwartz is a young New York designer whose wildly original clothes have been bought by women of high fashion and taste. Here is the artist modeling a coat that was on exhibit at the Museum of Contemporary Crafts' Baroque Show.

14

Bonnie Meltzer began crocheting on a life-sized scale when she created costumes for a children's play.

Julie Shaffler, shown here wearing a crocheted coat by Dina Schwartz, is not a crocheter herself; yet she deserves a place in the story of contemporary crochet for her development of a market for unusual, high fashion work. Her boutique on New York's fashionable Madison Avenue is a mecca for those who truly appreciate one-of-a-kind handmade clothes.

One wonders what a very proper Victorian like Mrs. Ann Stephens would have thought of a crocheter as informally dressed as Norma Minkowitz, shown relaxing in her stuffed and crocheted "Sensuous Chair."

Ron Goodman is another pioneer in sculptural crochet. In a statement accompanying his one-man crocheted sculpture show, the artist had this to say: "I am exploring the unknown qualities that make me what I am today. What you see is what I am, some of which I understand and much that I do not. It is as though (while working) I am overtaken by some unknown force that directs my mind/hand in producing the construction . . ." Photo by Link Harper.

Tools and Materials

2

The nineteenth-century crocheter's workbasket was apt to contain crochet hooks made out of ivory, bone, wood, or vulcanite. Beautiful hand-carved hooks are still available for collectors of unusual tools, but in general hooks actually in use are made of steel, aluminum, or plastic. The hooks come in different size ranges that are as yet not standardized for various materials. Plastic and aluminum hooks are sized by letters, steel hooks are sized by numbers. In the letter-sizing system the low letters of the alphabet represent the thinnest. The very fat hooks have higher letters, some as high (or as fat) as R and S. In the number sizing, the sequence from thin to fat is reversed, the higher the number, the thinner the hook. A 00, 0, or 1 hook is a large hook; a number 4 or 5 would be a thinner hook. All this won't be confusing if you merely hold different hooks against one another and compare them. It will soon become quite self-evident that a 0 steel hook is the equivalent of an E hook in aluminum.

Since hooks are very inexpensive and the only tools you really need, it's a good idea to buy hooks in a full range of sizes so that you have the right hook for the right project at your fingertips. Though plastic hooks tend to be somewhat cheaper than steel and aluminum, the difference in price is hardly worth the saving, if a saving it is, since the plastic hooks have a tendency to break and catch. A good minimum supply would be a C, a G, and an H aluminum hook with perhaps one #1 steel hook. (See Appendix.)

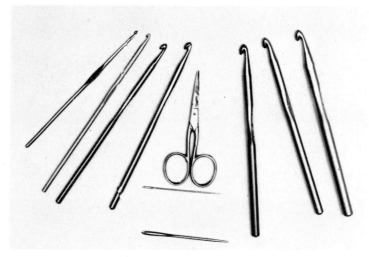

Hooks in various sizes plus embroidery needles for weaving in loose ends.

Hand-turned and -carved hardwood hooks for the collector. Photo courtesy Jules Kliot.

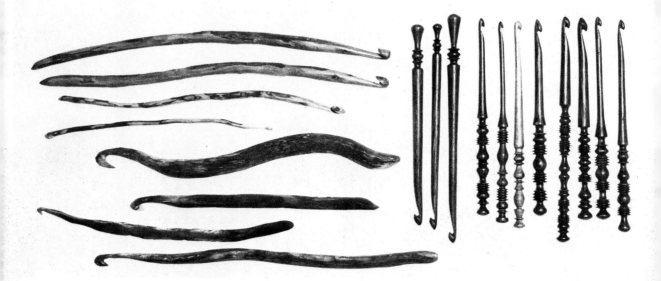

Some crocheters working with very heavy thick yarns like to fashion their own hooks, an easy enough project. Just buy a dowel stick of the desired width and length at the local hardware store. A hook then can be carved by hand or with an electric jigsaw if you have one.

An even more elementary sort of hook still used by some artists is the finger. This is great for very heavy yarns and for overcoming the beginner's confusion about holding yarn. Laurie Warner who teaches crochet always begins students with finger crochet since she feels it lets them immediately understand the structure and qualities of crochet. All artists working in finger crochet cite the intimacy and closeness this sort of contact provides.

Ron Goodman likes the intimacy of finger crochet. Photo Link Harper.

Laurie Warner starts her crochet students with finger crochet.

She has developed a variety of finger crochet stitches, but usually uses the basic one, which is structurally the same as the slip stitch used in hook crochet.

➤

Soft bag hangings by Laurie Warner. Mixed fibers worked in finger crochet. 14′ by 7′. Photo courtesy artist.

Detail of Laurie Warner's finger crochet hanging.

When to Use What Size Hook

The general rule about matching the right hook to the right yarn is easy and simple to remember: thin yarns for thin hooks, thick yarns for fat hooks. The best way to judge if you are using the right hook is from the way the yarn handles. If the yarn splits as it is pulled through or you have difficulty catching it in the hook, try another size.

Since in crochet some of the most interesting things happen when you break rules, try breaking the thin yarn-thin hook rule. Very unusual effects can be achieved by this rule-breaking. For example, by working a very thick yarn with a very thin hook you will achieve a particularly tight and solid texture, which may well be worth the strain this type of work puts on your fingers. On the other hand, by using a fairly heavy hook with a thin weaving yarn, you will be creating a lacy, open effect. Hook sizes can also be switched in the middle of a project, not only to change the effect of a pattern but, if need be, to correct mistakes. If, for example, your stitches are too loose, you can tighten them up by switching to a smaller hook, just as you can loosen up a too-tight stitch by going to a fatter hook.

Get the feel of different hooks with different yarns by working a patch in which you do two or three rows with one hook, two or three with another, and then trying still another.

Yarns

You can crochet with practically anything that can be wound around a crochet hook: string, rope, wool, acrylics, ribbon, chenille, plastic, metallics. To get started neither expensive nor esoteric yarns are needed.

Mary Lou Higgins, whose lovely work appears in several chapters, started crocheting as a child during the Depression. There was little money in the family for extras, and when her father found some boxes of red and brown string that had been thrown out of an overturned truck he brought them home. Mary Lou remembers crocheting with that string right through sixth grade. "Every time I didn't know what to do, I would sit down and crochet up some idea or need."

Helen Bitar uses mostly knitting worsted from the local five-and-ten-cent store to make her brilliant and free-spirited blankets. Some people can't use any kind of wool because of allergies; others are allergic to acrylics. If you're not sure about your material, hold a lighted match to the tip of a piece of yarn. Acrylic yarn will curl; wool will smell like burnt chicken feathers.

Many crocheters spin and dye their own wool. Most eventually fall in love with all types of fibers and become collectors. Del Pitt Feldman's yarn collection got so out of bounds that she ended up opening a yarn shop. Our own urge for real Mexican handspun fibers recently led us on an adventurous trip over unpaved roads into a still uncommercialized weaving village where we actually saw the sheep from which the lovely yarns we bought were shorn.

As you get more and more involved with crochet you too will want a

Yarns come in many thicknesses and textures, from fine cottons to heavy rug yarns.

variety of interesting yarns to work with at your disposal. In fact, after a while it can become something of the old story of the chicken and the egg for you may find yourself buying yarn not just to develop a particular idea but because the yarn itself strikes a cord within you, thus actually inspiring the project rather than the other way around. Whatever yarns you choose for your projects, be adventurous. Give even the most unlikely yarns a try. (See Appendix).

Cords, twines, raffia, are all suitable crochet materials. Cords and jutes are available in colors.

Ribbons of all sorts add contrast to crochet work. If possible, buy ribbons by the spools since they are too costly when bought by the yard.

Novelty yarns are the spice in a crocheter's supplies. Chenilles, velours, lurex, and curled wools are just some of the goodies worth searching out.

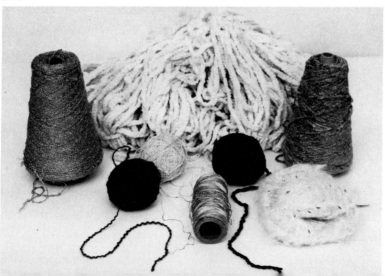

Using Textures Creatively

Most standard patterns for crochet items call for one type of wool to be used throughout. Part of the process of breaking free from the imitative is to combine your materials more freely. Try rough and coarse textures together; contrast thin against thick; zip up woolen areas with rows of shiny ribbon; edge a plain wool with a border of velour. Using plush, rich, and often expensive fibers as accents has the added advantage of enabling you to indulge a champagne taste even if you are on a limited budget.

Using Colors Creatively

Some artists, like Norma Minkowitz, prefer to work in white and off-white in order to explore the full potential of form and texture without relying on color. Others use color with wild abandon. Color is essentially a very personal thing and a sense for the "right" combination is something that most people develop by observation and experimentation more than by following set guide rules.

With yarns available in a truly breathtaking potpourri of colors the one rule that comes to mind is one of caution for the temptation to try everything at once, though strong, is best subdued. Use color, but always remember to use sufficient control so that everything works together harmoniously, rather than fighting for prominence of position. Tone down bold bright colors with some neutral tones. The best color scheme is that in which all the colors complement one another, and also the design. The best way for the crocheter to ensure a color scheme that will work well is to hold yarns next to each other to see how they really look side by side. For color scheme inspiration study paintings, nature, and fashions for ways in which colors can be harmoniously combined. Monochromatic schemes are particularly noteworthy for the crocheter who can use different shades of one color and also different textures within one shade. Don't overlook the noncolors: black and white and grays, alone or in combination with other colors; earth colors such as the ochres and ombres, which not only blend but will act as unifiers.

Other Tools and Materials

Though a crochet hook and yarn are truly all you need to get going, and keep going, there are some "extras."

Blocking Supplies

Some professional blockers have exaggerated the difficulties of this simple procedure so that most people are thoroughly intimidated about blocking their own work. All it really involves is pinning your work to a board, dampening it by applying a hot iron over a wet cloth, then letting it dry. Many things don't need to be blocked at all, and in fact should not be blocked. Most clothing items do benefit from blocking, and in many cases a good blocking can compensate for mistakes such as a sleeve being a bit small.

Your blocking board can be a large piece of plywood. Some people insist on a heavy piece of wood and nothing else. We've blocked successfully on sewing pattern boards and find our favorite blocking board to be a large poly-foam-backed paper board. In addition to the board, you need stainless steel t-pins such as those used to hold wigs to wig forms, a ruler, an iron, cotton cloths, towels and/or old blankets.

How to Block

As long as we're on the subject of blocking supplies, let's see exactly how blocking is done so that you can block any time the need arises.

1. Cover your board with a thick cloth or an old blanket.

2. Pin your crochet piece (it's easier to block pieces before they are sewn together) to the exact size you want. This is the time to stretch and widen if you wish. Be sure the pinheads are facing outward so they won't be in the way of the iron.

3. Wet a cloth and place over the work, then press your hot iron over the damp cloth. *Press, do not glide.* You are not ironing a handkerchief. What you want is to thoroughly dampen your work. If blocking a very large, three-dimensional piece, spray the surface with water instead of pressing with an iron.

4. Allow everything to dry *completely* before removing the pins.

5. For an extra thorough blocking, turn your work over and repeat the whole process for the other side.

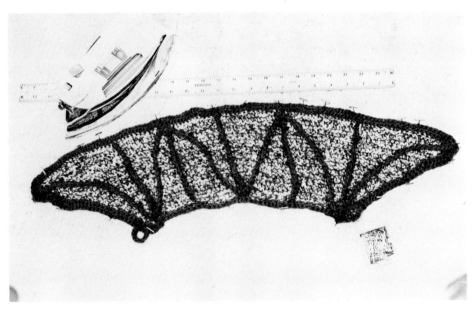

Block crochet pieces on a blanket-covered board. Make sure T pins are stainless steel and that the heads face outward, out of the way of the iron.

Stuffing

Whether or not you will be doing crochet sculpture or pillows, eventually you're going to make something that is stuffed. Washable acrylic stuffing is available in most notions stores. Save your old pantyhose, the bits of wool cut off when you wind off and change yarns and you'll have plenty of "found" stuffing. One of the best and most economical stuffings we've found is the lint that accumulates in your dryer. In case you didn't know it, lint allowed to accumulate is a severe fire hazard so be sure to remove it every second or third time you use your dryer, but save the lint in a big plastic bag and you will soon have a nice bag of soft, fluffy stuffing.

Miscellaneous

As you progress through the instructions that follow you will find that crochet can be combined with beads, leather, and all sorts of other materials. This is not so much a matter of buying additional supplies as finding new uses for things you are more than likely to have among your "useless" accumulations around the house. Thus, the only truly *must* tools and supplies for crocheting remain crochet hooks and yarns.

The Basis of it All:
The Chain Plus
the Versatile Single Crochet

3

All crochet stitches start from a basic chain that is in turn started with a slip-knot. Once you know how to make a chain and work your way back along the chain you will know how to crochet. It's that simple, really!

Of course, at the beginning you will take this statement with more than a grain of salt. Learning to manipulate your needle and yarn will make you feel about as nimble-fingered as an elephant. You'll tend to grasp the hook too tightly. The yarn will slip off your fingers. Take heart, however. Feeling clumsy is a phase through which the most experienced crocheter has gone and phases are always temporary. Yours will probably last as long as it takes you to make a long crochet chain and work back along it.

The following demonstrations are based on what we've found to be the most popular and easiest methods for handling and holding hooks and yarn. If you find your way of working does not quite match the photos, don't feel you've gone off. Your method may indeed be better. The emphasis in this book is on individuality and this applies to methods as well as results.

All stitch demonstrations are made with cotton and rayon rug yarn and an aluminum G hook. Our choice was based largely on the fact that these made the clearest photos. The illustrations are all based on right-handed crocheting. Many left-handed crocheters seem to be able to crochet as "righties." You can also reverse directions visually by holding a mirror over the illustrations.

Holding Your Hook

Every crochet hook has a fingerhold that may be grasped in an overhand manner or from underneath, like a pencil. The pencil hold looks a bit more graceful but most people find the overhand hold more comfortable.

Pencil hold, once considered the "best" way to hold crochet hook.

Overhand hold, the most popular hold today; it gives a firmer grip, especially when working with heavy yarns.

Making a Slipknot

Hold the short end of the yarn in the left hand and bring the long end around the loop as shown.

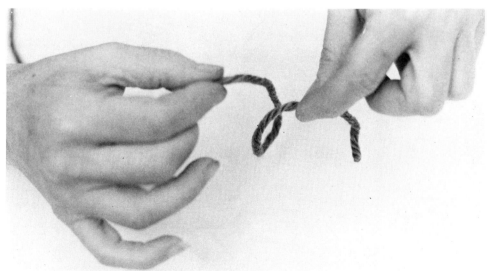

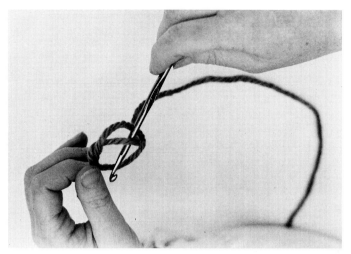

Let the long end of the yarn form a vertical bar across the loop and pull this through with your hook.

Tighten the loop that locks in the stitch. Don't pull *too* tight, or leave *too* loose.

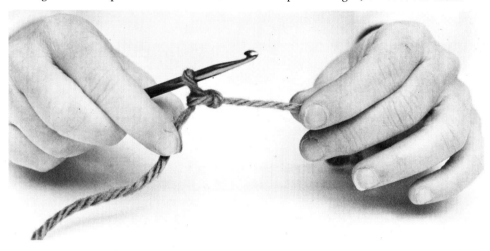

Making the Chain

Loop the yarn around your left hand as shown. The left hand holding the yarn also controls the tension.

Bring the yarn from the yarn-holding hand over and in front of the loop on the hook and pull through. Pattern directions call this "yarn over," or "yoh." Be sure your hook is pointed in the direction of the loop so that you can pull the yarn through in one motion.

Keep bringing the yarn in front of the hook and pull it through the loop. It's a good idea to hold the beginning of your chain between the thumb and forefinger to keep it from turning and curling.

Crochet Chain Projects

The chain is primarily a steppingstone, the base on which all other crochet stitches are built. Yet, it is not without its completely independent uses.

Crochet chains can be twisted and bent into all sorts of chains that can then be sewn to other fabrics with simple overhand sewing stitches. By combining chains in different colors and yarns, a variety of embroidery effects can be achieved. The technique is very reminiscent of the yarn paintings made popular by Mexican folk artists. During a recent trip to Mexico we noticed that many of the popular yarn and string designs had been enriched by the use of a chain rather than an unchained strand of yarn. Some of the Mexican crochet chain designs were glued in place but the better, more expensive items were all stitched.

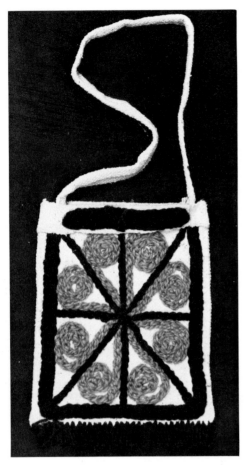

Mexican linen bag, decorated with crochet chain embroidery.

A simple sweater is accented with wool and mohair crochet in three different colors.

Crochet chain lion design on felt pillow cover. Arden Newsome.

The Single Crochet

All crochet stitches are really just variations of the single crochet so it is indeed the single most important stitch. Whole garments and hangings and sculptures can be made using just the single crochet stitch.

Let's do a row of single crochet stitches off the base or foundation chain, and then make a second row of single crochets.

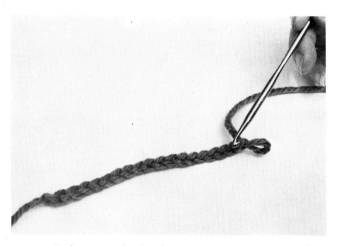

Before you begin, learn to count your stitches. This chain has 18 stitches. The slipknot at the base of the chain is not counted as a stitch. The hook has been removed to point to the second chain. This is your first stitch. Depending on which way the chain faces you when you crochet, you will insert the hook under the top two crossed loops, or into the top single strand of your first stitch.

Insert your hook, yarn over, and pull through the first loop.

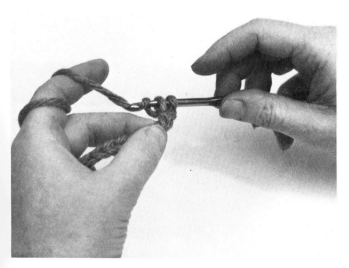

Yarn over again and pull through the two remaining loops.

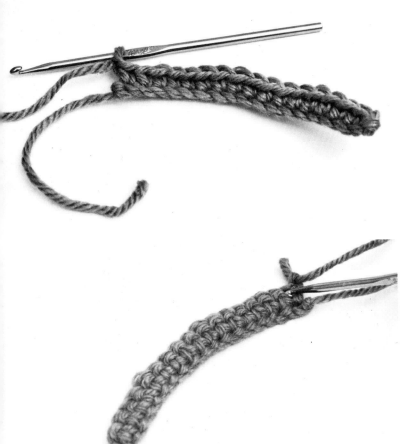

Here is the completed row of singles. Each stitch ends with a single loop on the hook.

Before turning your work around for the next row, make an extra chain. This is called Chain 1 (Chapter 1). The purpose of this step is to bring the turning chain up to the height of the stitches of the next row. When you learn to make taller stitches, you will be making taller turning chains, but the important thing to remember is that you must make a turning chain and *the turning chain counts as the first stitch of the next row.*

Here is your row of single crochets turned into position for row two. The hook is removed to clearly point out the second stitch of the row (remember, your turning chain counts as the first stitch). In actual practice, the hook is not removed when turning; instead the work is flipped around in counterclockwise motion.

Single Crochet Variations

The next photo series shows how, by varying the method of inserting the hook into the stitch, different patterns can be achieved.

The regular single crochet is made by inserting the hook through the two top loops of the previous stitch.

Sample of regular single crochet stitches.

By inserting the hook only through the front loop of the previous stitch a variation known as the rose stitch is made.

Sample of rose stitch.

Inserting the hook through the back loop of the previous stitch raises a ridged pattern, and so the name ridge stitch.

Ridge stitch sample.

Still another way to vary your regular single crochet is to insert the hook through both loops as for the regular single, but yarn over from back to front. This creates a cross-stitch pattern.

Cross-stitch sample.

Skills with Your Stitches

In order to turn your newly acquired stitch know-how into finished projects, you will want to learn some additional techniques such as ending off, changing yarns, and connecting one piece of crochet to another. Along with these basics, it's fun to learn some nonessential skills such as crocheting in beads, which can add considerable zip and style to your work.

Ending Off

Ending off in crochet is so simple that most people figure it out before anyone can show it to them.

Cut the yarn leaving a length of about 6 inches; yarn over and pull through.

Pull the end out, then pull tight. Thread the loose end onto an embroidery needle and weave in and out of the back of the work.

Changing Yarn

If you keep your first projects small you could probably complete them with a single ball of wool. Why not get right into the excitement of alternating colors, though? The easiest way to change colors is to go to the end of the row. Instead of completing the last stitch, cut the yarn, leaving a length of about six inches. Tie your new yarn close to the loops on the hooks; then finish your stitch in the new color.

Cut your old yarn before completing your last stitch and tie the new color close to the remaining two loops.

Complete the stitch with the new yarn and chain to turn.

As you start your next row, crochet the ends of the yarn right into the work, thus weaving your loose ends into the work automatically.

Connecting Pieces of Crochet

You can connect pieces by sewing them together with a simple overhand stitch. When using the sewing method, place the pieces together so that the right sides face inward. You can also crochet your pieces together with a slip stitch, which is a shorter version of the single crochet and used primarily for this purpose or as an edging stitch. To make a slip stitch: 1. Insert the hook and yarn over exactly as you would for a single crochet. 2. Pull the yarn through both loops at once. In other words, skip the second yarn over.

A third method of connecting two pieces of crochet is to have the right sides of the pieces facing out and single crocheting along the edges. This raises a ridge along the connected edge, which is often very attractive and desirable.

Single Crochet Plus Basic Skills Project: A Purse Belt

The best way to really practice stitches and skills is to actually make something as you go along. The more you work, the more your enthusiasm will grow. You'll soon discover that even the simplest projects look great. As you gain courage from experience, your beginning projects can grow in any direction you wish. Your first belt may well lead to a magnificent hanging.

The belt is a sampler of the single crochet and its variations and offers practice in combining and changing colors and connecting pieces of crochet. To make the belt:

1. Make a chain that measures scantily around your hips or waist, depending on how you wear the belt. The scanty fit allows for the stretch factor.

2. Use three different colors and do two rows in each color. Use a different single crochet for each color . . . two rows in the ridge stitch, two rows in the rose stitch, and two in the cross-stitch.

3. Crochet all around the belt with a regular single crochet. Make three stitches into each corner for a nice sharp turn.

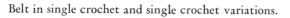

Belt in single crochet and single crochet variations.

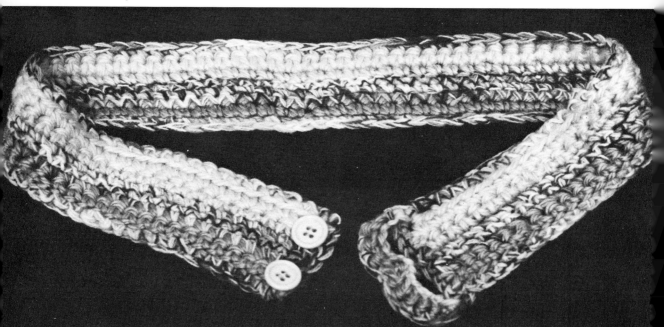

4. To make loops for the buttons, single crochet along the short end of the belt. Do one or two stitches, then chain up two or three stitches and skip a corresponding number of stitches for the loop. Crochet a stitch and then chain up and skip stitches for the second loop. This is how all buttonholes are made. To give body to the button loops, crochet back over the loops for two or three more rows.

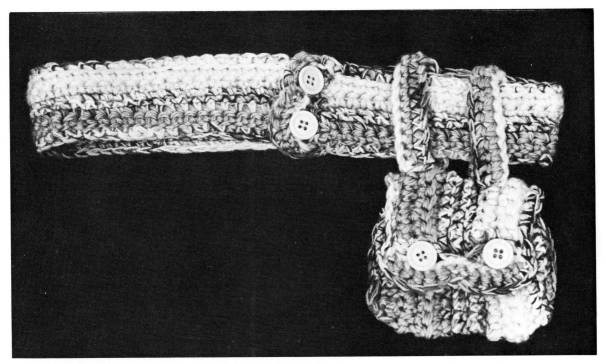

Here is the belt complete with belt-looper purse. The purse is a straight piece of crochet. It's folded into thirds and the two bottom thirds are crocheted together on the outside with a single crochet stitch. The closing loops are made exactly like the button loops of the belt.

More Special Skills

Beads go so well with crochet that to many creative crocheters they are an integral part of their work. If beads are an afterthought, they can be sewn in place after your design is complete. However, you can crochet them right into the work very simply and easily. There are two methods of doing this:

1. String your beads right into the crochet yarn and as you need a bead let it slip down right next to your crochet hook and crochet around it. The bead will fall to the back of the work so it's best to work in beads from the back side so they will fall to the front. A word of warning: Always string more beads than you think you need if you want to avoid having to break your thread, restring, and tie on anew.

Your use of crocheting beads may be somewhat limited by the fact that your beads must have a hole large enough for the yarn to pass through. The yarn tip can be considerably thinned and stiffened for easy threading by waxing with beeswax or sculptor's wax.

The beads are strung onto the yarn, and as a bead is needed, it is slipped down right next to the crochet hook. The stitch is made around the bead. The bead will fall to the back of the stitch so it's easiest to work beads from the back side in order to have them fall to the front. Otherwise, they can be pushed to the front.

One yarn and a piece of beeswax showing how the waxing can refine the tip for easier threading.

2. The second method for beading permits you to use even tiny beads with very fat yarns. In this case the beads are strung onto nylon monafilament fishing line. The beaded monafilament is tied to the yarn and carried along the back of the crochet work. Whenever you want a bead, just drop it against the hook. The nylon is invisible. This method is demonstrated in the beaded bag project that follows.

Making a Beaded Bag

Here's another useful practice project. The sample is made in cross-stitch crochet, with cotton and rayon rug yarn, black wool for the edging. The rug yarn makes for a strong firm texture. The beading is done at the edgings and could be eliminated. The basic bag consists of a simple rectangle. You can mix stitches as well as colors. Since the rug yarn is strong, a lining is not essential but it makes for a nicer looking, more finished bag. If you use felt, you can glue or sew the lining, though we recommend sewing.

The bag is a cross-stitched rectangle. Five stitches were chained and then skipped in the center of the next-to-the-last row to make an opening for a closing flap. This is the same method used for making buttonholes. A piece of felt, a bit smaller than the outside of the bag, will be used as a lining.

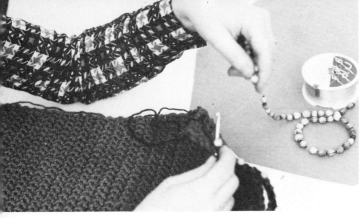

Beads are strung onto monofilament.

The beaded nylon thread is carried along in back of the crochet work and a bead is slipped down and crocheted in place about every fifth stitch.

The bag is sewn together at the sides and an extra strip of cross stitches is sewn in place as a closing flap. Unless you line your handle, make it shorter than needed to allow for the stretch factor.

The finished bag, simple and attractive and uniquely yours. Since economy is no minor matter in today's expensive world it might be interesting to note that the entire bag cost approximately a dollar to make. Of course, costlier yarn, lining fabrics, and beads could bring the price up.

How to Cover a Ring with Crochet

So far you've been too involved with getting used to what to do with your yarn and hook to give much thought to self-expression. Now that you're familiar with basic crocheting and have made some simple and practical project, it's time to start working in a more spontaneous way. A good exercise for free-form crochet is to crochet around a ring or a frame and then doodle within that frame to create random shapes and spaces. Discarded bicycle rims, hoops, or frames are great. As you will see from some of the illustrations the results can be beautiful and well worth mounting and hanging.

Once you learn to crochet around a large ring, you will find many adaptations for this technique. Small rings make handsome pendants and necklaces.

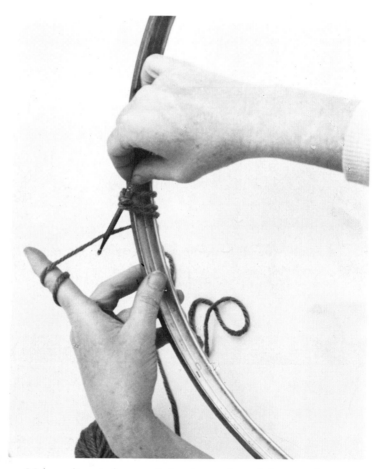

Make a slip stitch around the ring and catch loop as shown.

Complete your stitch and keep covering the ring, moving the stitches closely together for a completely wrapped look.

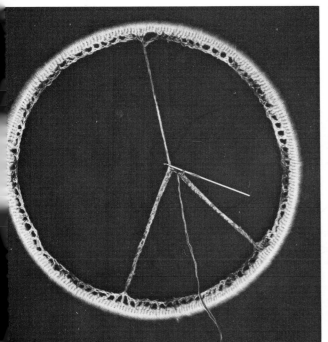

The stitches from which you will work your design can be turned inside the ring, or kept at the outside. To get your designs going, work some chains back and forth across the ring.

Work back across some of the chains.

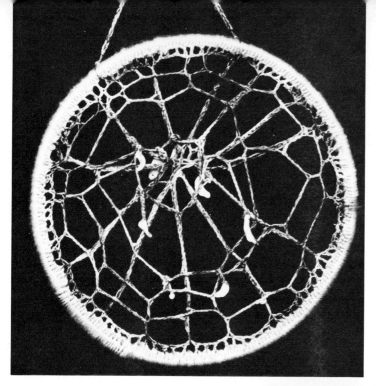

You can make a very simple design by working around and around, always attaching stitches to the crossbars. Shells were added to the illustrated design. The pattern is worked from the outside to the center.

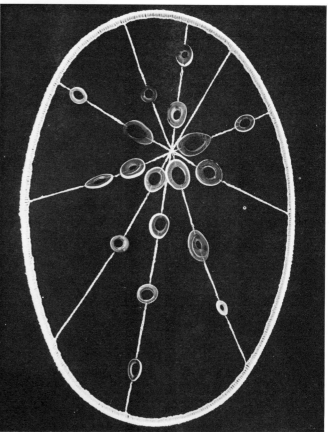

Le Jeune Whitney works her beads into the basic crossbars . . .

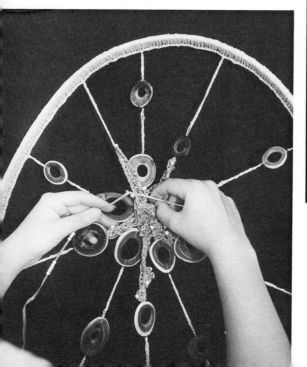

. . . then crochets in between the large beads, adding smaller ones as she goes along.

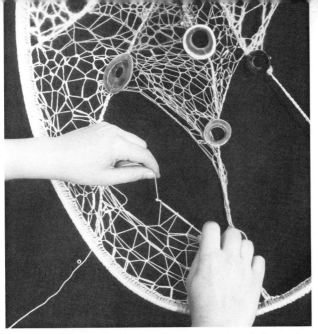

The open netting effect is continued from the center out to the edge of the ring.

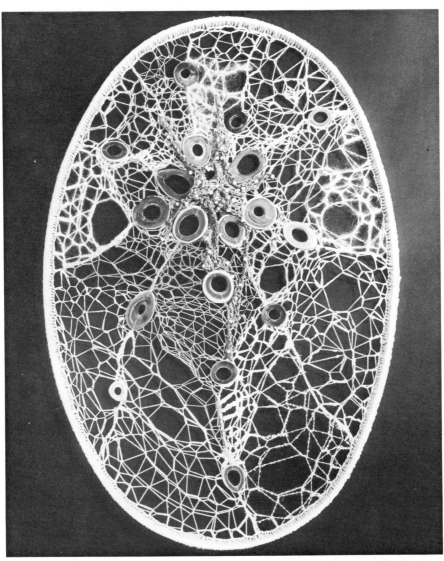

The finished web. Photo courtesy artist.

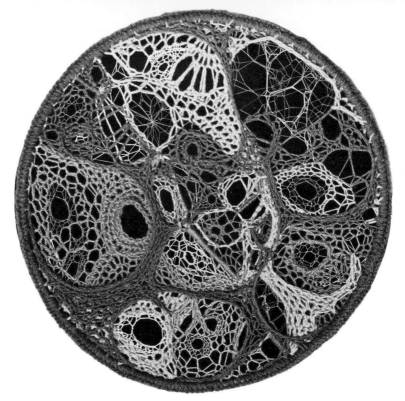

Madge Copeland mixes a variety of yarns and works in some wrapping. The finished ring is mounted on a velvet-covered board. Photo courtesy artist.

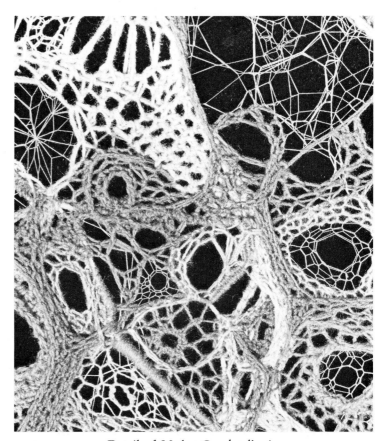

Detail of Madge Copeland's ring.

Ruth Walters likes to start her rings by crocheting some amorphous-shaped pieces and then stretching them into her stitch-covering ring. (See color section for another ring.) Photo courtesy artist.

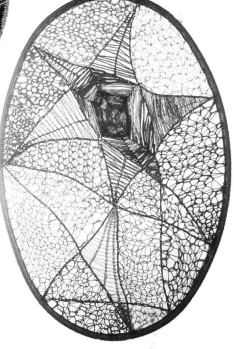

Le Jeune Whitney wrapped synthetic rayon straw over and under the central portion of this web to create an Ojo de dios design, showing that there are indeed no limits to the possibilities for this type of free-form crochet. Photo courtesy artist.

Though round and oval rings are easiest to cover, square and rectangular shapes can be used for these free-form designs. This crocheted frame was mounted on a mirror which reflected the back of the design adding an extra dimension.

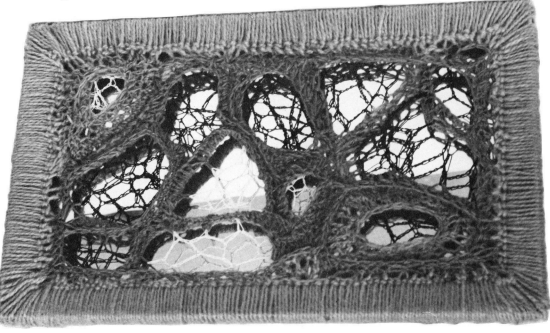

Translating Those Funny Symbols into More Basic Stitches and Skills: The Tall Stitches

4

HDC, DC, TR, INC, DEC, * . . . Looking at some of the standard stitch-by-stitch crochet patterns seems more like an invitation to crack a secret code than directions for crocheting. Don't let the abbreviations and asterisks that dot these patterns scare you off, though. HDC stands for a half double crochet stitch; DC for a double crochet, TR for a triple crochet; Inc and Dec mean increasing and decreasing; the asterisk indicates the beginning and end of a pattern. Any instructions given outside the asterisk marks are followed just once, whereas those within the asterisk marks are repeated. To further confuse readers of both British and American patterns the British call the North American single crochet a double crochet; the half double, a half treble; and the double, a treble. (See Appendix.)

In the following pages you will learn to actually translate all these terms into stitches and techniques. The additional stitches are really more variations of the basic single crochet. By looping your yarn around the hook more often than with the single crochet you are simply building a taller version of the basic single. Taller stitches tend to be more open and lacier. By knowing how to vary the sizes of your stitches you will also have more control over the shape of your work.

The stitches will be demonstrated in order of height progression. Each is worked on a base chain with a row of single crochets worked back along the chain. This tends to give a firmer foundation row but is not an unbreakable rule.

Half Double Crochet (HDC)

The half double is just a little taller than the single crochet. It is used much less than its shorter cousin the single, or its taller cousins the double and treble crochets. However, though it isn't popular as a stitch to be used for whole stretches of crochet work, it is an extremely useful utilitarian stitch. It can compensate just the right amount in areas where you need a bit of extra height without wanting the change to show up abruptly.

Chain two stitches and turn your work. The two turning chains count as your first two stitches. The row is begun by inserting the hook into the chain next to the turning chain. In the photo, the hook is removed from the work and used merely as a pointer so you can see clearly where to begin your row.

To make the half double crochet, bring your yarn over before inserting the hook.

Yarn over in front of the three loops on the hook and pull through all three loops.

This leaves you with one loop and the completed half double crochet.

Double Crochet (DC)

This is a still taller stitch so you must start with an even taller chain.

Chain 3 to turn. Start the row again by inserting the hook into the chain next to the turning chain. Thus, when the patterns instruct you to insert your hook into the 4th chain, they mean the three turning chains plus the next one over.

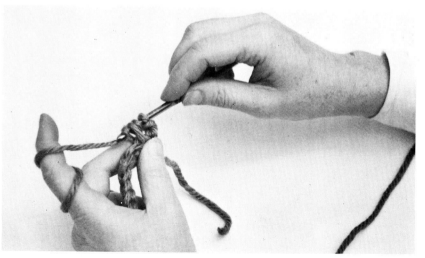

To make the double crochet, yarn over, insert your hook, and yarn over in front of the three loops. This is exactly what you did for the half double crochet.

48

Pull the yarn through two of the three loops only, leaving two on the hook. Now yarn over before these remaining two loops as shown in the photo.

Yarn through the remaining two loops and your double crochet is complete.

Treble Crochet (TC)

By this time you can probably guess that this stitch is going to be even taller than the double.

Chain up 4. (Your first stitch is still the one next to this turning chain.) Now yarn over *two times* before inserting your hook into the loop.

Here are the four loops you will have on the hook after this first step of yarning over twice and inserting the hook into the next loop.

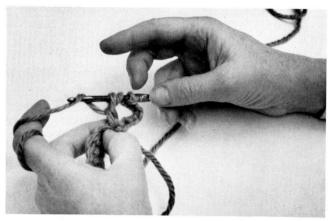

Bring the yarn before the four loops and pull through two. You will have three loops left as shown. Bring your yarn over before the three loops and . . .

. . . pull through two more loops, leaving you with two loops on the hook. Yarn over before the remaining two loops, pull through . . .

. . . and your treble crochet is complete.

Samples of single crochets, double crochets, and treble crochets showing the difference in height between the stitches. The slip stitch is even shorter than the single, and the double treble continues the height progression from the treble.

For an even shorter stitch you can use the slip stitch described in Chapter 3. For a still taller stitch than the treble you could make a double treble. This calls for a turning chain of 5, yarning over 3 times and then continuing to work off the 5 loops, two at a time.

Half Doubles, Doubles, and Trebles Without Base Rows

If you decide to start your tall stitches directly from your chain, without a base row of singles, you will not have a turning chain but will have to compensate for the height of your stitches by actually skipping chains. Here's how this would work:

HALF DOUBLE CROCHET: Instead of chaining 2, go into the third chain from the loop.

DOUBLE CROCHET: Instead of chaining 3, go into the fourth chain from the loop.

TREBLE CROCHET: Instead of chaining 4, go into the fifth chain from the loop.

Skills for Your Stitches: Increasing and Decreasing

There are two more absolutely vital skills you will need to master if you want to go beyond making straight projects. The ability to increase and decrease is the key to adding shape and contour to the things you make. Each is as easy as it is necessary.

Increases are made quite simply by making two stitches into one. Gradual increases are made by increasing at the beginning of every row. It's neater to increase into the second stitch rather than the first.

To increase a lot, as for a collar or a cape, work out a pattern of increases all across a row . . . an increase every third stitch, every sixth stitch, or whatever is called for. We find increases are smoother if a row of increases is alternated with a row of straight crocheting.

By increasing constantly into every stitch, at times even going more than twice into the same stitch, you can create wonderful-looking ruffles.

A machine-knit sweater gets a new look with a collar made by working a row of single crochets all around the neckline and then crocheting back and forth along the row with lots of increases, three or four into one stitch, all around.

To Decrease Stitches

You could simply skip a stitch to decrease but this will leave a hole. It is neater and just as easy to decrease by making half a stitch and then going on to the next stitch.

For a single crochet decrease insert your hook, yarn over, and pull through. Instead of completing the stitch by yarning over and pulling through the two loops on the hook . . .

. . . go on to the next stitch, yarn over and pull through all three loops. You have combined two stitches.

Decreasing Taller Stitches

The same method used to decrease single crochets works with the taller stitches. Here's how this works out:

DOUBLE CROCHET: Yarn over, insert hook into loop, yarn over and pull through two loops. This is half a stitch, leaving two loops on the hook. Instead of working these off, go to the next double. Work off the first two loops of the second double, which will leave you with three loops on the hook. Complete your combined or decreased double by yarning through all three loops at once.

TRIPLE CROCHET: Yarn over two times, insert hook, yarn over and pull through two loops. Complete another portion of the stitch by yarning over and pulling through two more loops. Now, with two loops from the first treble remaining on your hook, yarn over two times and go onto your next stitch. Work this off until you have three loops left, as with the double, and pull through *all three* loops to complete your combined or decreased treble.

Learning to Be Free with the Use of Increases and Decreases

Now that you can shape your crochet work to go in and out rather than just straight up and down, you can achieve any shape you wish. Try it out by drawing some free-form doodles on a sheet of paper and see if you can follow the outline of the doodle. The vest on page 130 grew out of just such a doodle. An amorphous shape was drawn. Stitches were cast on to match the straight top. The bell-like center was developed with gradual increases, the rounded bottom with gradual decreases.

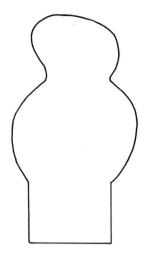

Try following an amorphous shape like this with increases and decreases as you go along, always holding your work against the outline of your shape. Once you learn to make rounds and ovals (Chapter 6), you will have still other methods for working out shapes.

Making a Halter

Now that you know how to increase and decrease you're ready to make your first item of clothing. The illustrated halter is made in all single crochets but you could work it in some other stitches. Taller stitches would give more of a see-through look. This is another good opportunity to work with lots of different colors. Pick at least three. Use one color as an accent by working it for only one row at a time; give prominence to another by working it in for three or four consecutive rows. The halter is a backless, sleeveless garment that keeps fit and construction very simple, with just enough shaping at the front to give you practice in decreasing.

Cast on enough stitches to barely go around your waist or that of whoever is going to wear it. The snug fit is to allow for the stretch factor present in all crochet work.

Crochet a straight piece until it measures just below your armhole.

The shaped portion of the halter is worked separately. Tie a string at each side where the armhole begins. Start each side at the closing and crochet

Striped halter crocheted and designed by Lorraine Bodger and Delia Brock.

only as far as the string marker. At the marker, chain up and turn. Decrease a stitch at the beginning of each row at the armhole side and keep going for as high as you want the halter to be. The other shaped side is worked to match.

For a snugly fitted and very decorative waist, crochet a very long chain and weave it in and out of the bottom of the halter.

Working Three-Dimensionally

Soon you will see how crochet can be worked in circles and tubes, stuffed and built around armatures in order to create sculptural effects. You can create three-dimensional forms right now, simply by picking up stitches from the surface of your crochet fabric and building ridged patterns and designs. Tie some yarn anywhere along the top of your work and single crochet in any direction you want. Let's see how this is done with another easy beginning project.

Making a Three-Dimensional Scarf Collar

The sample was made with two shades of knitting worsted (beige and brown) stranded together and worked as one. We used an aluminum G hook.

Stitches are cast on in a chain long enough to just fit around the neck. To give the collar sufficient flare a pattern of increasing all across every other row was worked out. In the illustrated collar, an increase was made in every sixth stitch. This can vary with the wool used and the fullness desired. The best way to judge is to keep holding the collar on yourself and trying it as you go along.

For the edging, the brown yarn was doubled and single crochets were made all around. The button loop is a small chain.

The raised design is made by crocheting lines of single crochets back and forth across the surface.

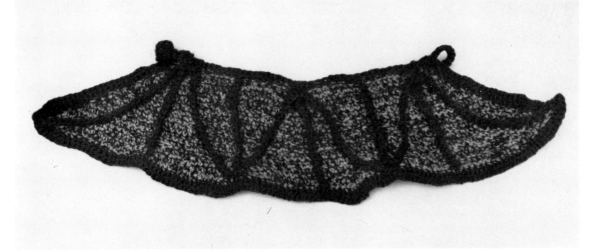

The finished collar, which could easily grow into a cape.

Another view of the three-dimensional collar. The beret is crocheted in raffia by Alison Schiff.

These beautiful forms crocheted onto a 4 by 5 foot woolen hanging dramatically illustrate the potential of the simple three-dimensional technique just learned. Mary Stephens Nelson used a warm gray and black for her Moon Blanket, which is owned by the Boise Cascade Corporation. Photo by Tom Henscheid.

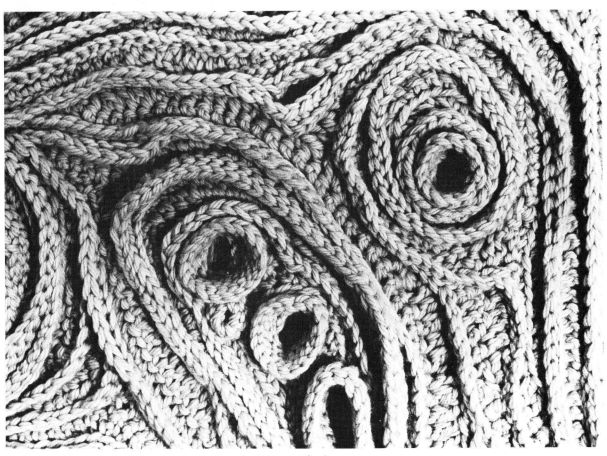

Detail of Moon Blanket.

Three-dimensional designs can be further shaped and ruffled by making lots of increases into the stitches you make on the surface. Jeff Berman, artist and photographer.

Random Stitch Hanging

The size contrasts between single crochet and taller stitches can be used creatively to obtain unusual visual effects. Le Jeune Whitney crocheted a variety of yarns in white-beige-pale yellows into bands of single, half double, double, and treble crochet stitches. Five vertical groups of stitches were joined and the loose yarn ends worked into fabric bands, which were then made into tubes through which brass rods were slipped to give support and weight to the hanging. The use of open spaces and inclusion of fluffy mohair all work to carry through the artist's concept of free-form clouds.

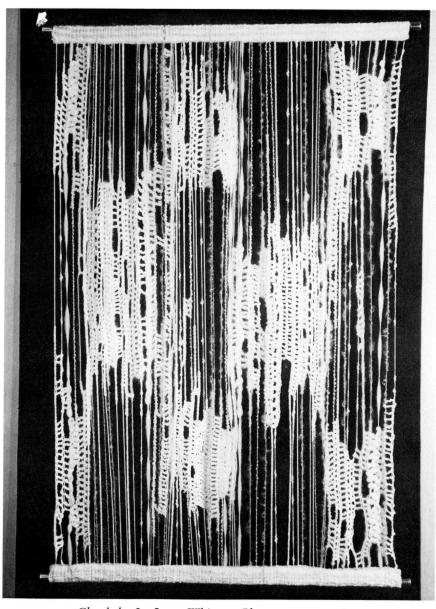

Clouds by Le Jeune Whitney. Photo courtesy artist.

Getting Fancy: The Most Popular and Useful Accent Stitches

5

Fancy stitches add lovely textural accents to your work. Although some of them may look complicated at first, they're really just pattern variations of your single and double crochet stitch. By working the basic stitches in different patterns, you can create shells, meshes, loops, and bumps. There are literally hundreds of stitches and stitch variations that have been passed on from crocheter to crocheter. Whole books have been compiled that are devoted exclusively to patterns. Mary Dawson's *Complete Guide to Crochet Stitches* illustrates seventeen variations of the shell stitch alone. We've chosen examples of the most versatile and popular stitches. You can invent variations of your own or refer to some of the pattern books if you wish to increase your range of stitch vocabulary.

The Shell Stitch

The shell is probably the most popular of all crochet stitches. The following demonstration for a simple closed shell is made on a base chain of 20 stitches that makes the pattern work out just right for the beginning and ending on a half shell.

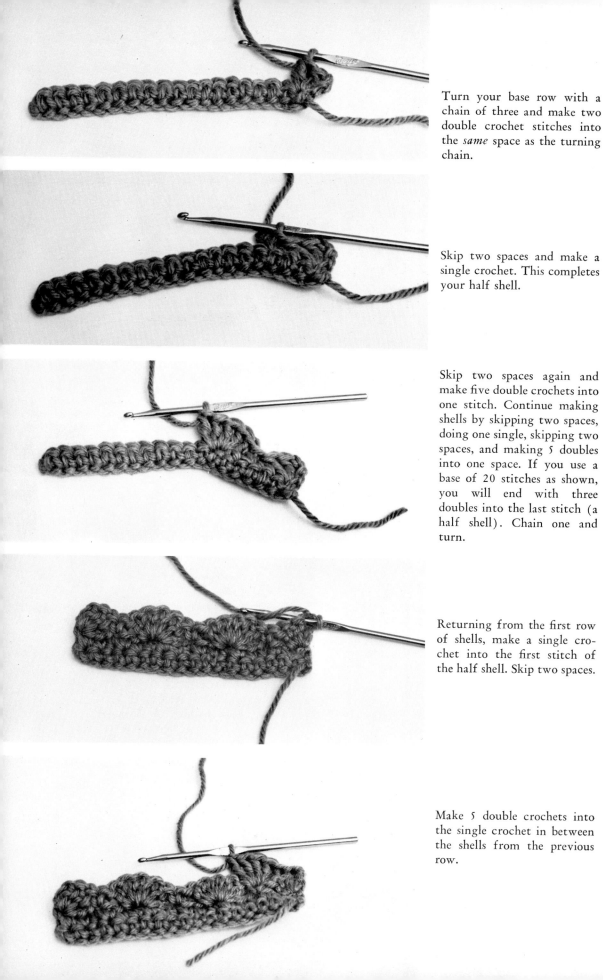

Turn your base row with a chain of three and make two double crochet stitches into the *same* space as the turning chain.

Skip two spaces and make a single crochet. This completes your half shell.

Skip two spaces again and make five double crochets into one stitch. Continue making shells by skipping two spaces, doing one single, skipping two spaces, and making 5 doubles into one space. If you use a base of 20 stitches as shown, you will end with three doubles into the last stitch (a half shell). Chain one and turn.

Returning from the first row of shells, make a single crochet into the first stitch of the half shell. Skip two spaces.

Make 5 double crochets into the single crochet in between the shells from the previous row.

A lacy open shell made circa 1930 and still worn today by its owner, Rhoda Shiffreen.

Cluster Stitches

Fat stitches that pop out from a flat design are very useful for lending extra texture and dramatic accent. All are made by a process of clustering groups of stitches together. Each of the following stitches achieves its fullness in a somewhat different way.

Basic Cluster Stitch

Chain 3 and make half complete double crochets into the third chain until you have 5 loops on the hook.

Yarn over and pull through all 5 loops. Chain one to lock in your stitch.

Pineapple Stitch

This is a puffier version of the basic cluster. The doubles are not even half completed. The yarn is just pulled up on the hook.

Chain 3, yarn over, insert the hook and yarn through (3 loops on hook). Repeat this 3 more times so that you have the original loop plus 8 other loops on your hook as shown.

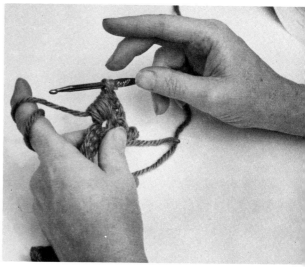

Yarn through 8 loops. You will have two loops left.

Yarn through the remaining two loops and chain one.

Popcorn Stitch

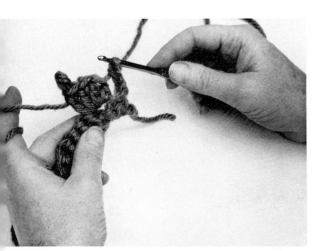

Chain 3 and do 4 doubles into the same space as the turning chain. Take the hook out of the last loop as shown.

Insert your hook into the third chain of the cluster.

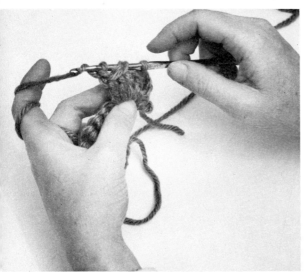

Reinsert your hook, yarn over and pull through two loops.

Yarn through the remaining loops and chain one. Skip a space before making your next popcorn.

Cluster, pineapple, and popcorn stitch sample, showing the variations between the different types of clusters.

Loop Stitch

This is a very useful stitch for hangings, to create hair, furlike fluffiness, rug textures. The demonstration shows the loop made over the forefinger of the right hand. You may prefer looping over the left hand. You can also use a ruler or cardboard as a looper to assure complete evenness. The stitch is the same regardless of the procedural details. Since the loops fall to the back of the work, the stitch is worked from the back to the front, on one side only.

Insert hook into stitch and loop around the finger once or twice, depending upon the desired length of the loop.

Hold onto the loop as shown and complete your stitch. Then drop the loop.

The loops fall in back of the stitch so it's usually worked from back to front only.

Loop stitch sample.

Pattern Stitches

Filet crochet is really a process of creating a pattern and not a stitch at all. The pattern is created by spacing stitches to create various open-mesh designs. The tapestry stitch is again crocheting in a pattern. Colors are worked into single crochet work like needlepoint designs.

Straight Filet Pattern

To make a basic box pattern, chain 3, skip one stitch, and make a double crochet . . . chain one, skip one stitch, and make a double crochet. Keep chaining, skipping, and crocheting. The chain takes the place of the space you skip and creates the mesh. You can come back on the first row of doubles so that the spaces are directly over one another with the bars touching, or alternate the pattern by having the bar in the middle of the stitch. Patterns can be varied by using taller stitches and making larger meshes, or you can go free-form by chaining and skipping at random to create a completely uneven mesh pattern.

Boxy filet pattern sample. This one is worked by chaining two stitches and skipping two stitches.

Arch stitch filet pattern made by doing a single crochet into the third chain, chaining 5, missing 3 chains, and doing a single into the next stitch. On the return row, a single crochet is made into the center of the 5 chain loop.

Tapestry Pattern Stitch

This is a way of working color designs right into a piece of single crochet. One or two colors in addition to the background color are carried along at the back of the work and are picked up when the pattern calls for them. Any tapestry type of needlework design can be adapted to tapestry stitch crochet, or your own design can be charted out on graph paper. Tapestry crocheting tends to go more slowly because of the need to work in a controlled pattern and the constant switching of the yarns. However, the yarns crocheted along the back like this give a lovely and distinctive texture to this type of pattern, which is well worth the effort.

Try your hand at tapestry with a simple box pattern, working four or five stitches in each of two colors.

Start the pattern by tying in the new color before finishing your stitch.

Finish the stitch by yarning through the new color.

Continue to crochet in the new color, carrying the original color in back and crocheting it right into the fabric. Keep the balls of yarn spread out in front of you.

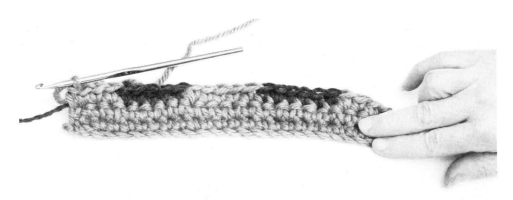

The box pattern begins to take shape. The tapestry pattern is easiest when used as a border where the work goes around and doesn't need turning. However, you can work the tapestry on both sides if you are careful to pull the thread that is being carried firmly through your stitches.

A dainty cotton purse in pink and green tapestry, bought in Paris and lent by Sharon Hedges. Note the little shells on the bottom.

Fancy Finishes

A really lovely piece of crochet can be spoiled by the one missing link that would make a truly fine finished work, namely, a nice edging. An edging does not have to be fancy. Some things call for a plain tailored edge, which is best achieved with a row of slip stitches or single crochets. Sometimes something a little different is called for. A row of shell or popcorn stitches can be used as fancy edgings. A small scallop often looks better than the larger shell, though, and the tiny bump made by a picot better than the more prominent popcorn. A corded edge is tailored like slip stitches but a bit more distinctive. It's also good for giving an extra weight to the bottom of a scarf or a cape. All edgings can be used within a piece of crochet too.

To make a picot edging:

Chain 3 and go back into the same space as the chain with a slip stitch. This forms a little bump. You can space out your picots with one or two or more single crochets in between each one.

To make a scallop edging:

Chain 3 and make a double crochet into the same space, then skip two stitches.

Finished scallops look like miniature shell stitches.

To make a corded edge:

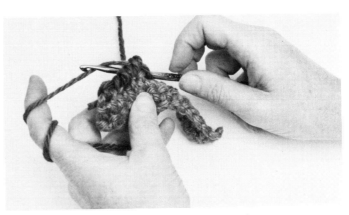

This is a regular single crochet, except that it's worked from *left* to *right*. Insert the needle from front to back and grab hold of the yarn as shown.

Yarn through to complete the stitch.

Samplers of Fancy Stitches

Many crocheters have happily discovered that even their first samplers look attractive and are well worth keeping, specially if mounted in an interesting way and embellished with a few finishing touches.

Elyse Sommer's first crochet sampler. Yellow, white, blue, and brown wool are worked in a pattern of single, double, and treble crochets, interspersed with rows of arch stitches and finished with three rows of loop stitches. To keep it all from looking too symmetrical and sampler-like, an uneven picot edge was worked along each side. A piece of driftwood and driftwood dangles complete the hanging.

Alison Schiff experimented with raffia and twine, tufting out some of the edges. It's mounted on a crossbar of wood.

The centerpiece of this hanging is a sampler of fancy stitches. It affords an exercise in increasing and decreasing to create an amorphous shape. Several other amorphous shapes were made. Raised designs were added to each piece at random. The forms were then tied into a discarded bicycle rim which was wrapped in black cord to match the edgings of the pieces. The dangles are brass washers. Study in Black, White, and Red.

Chapter 8 will be devoted entirely to clothing, including instructions for making and following patterns. However, following are some examples of clothing that require no clothes-making know-how but do afford a chance to use fancy stitches.

Fancy Stitch Shawls

You can edge a fabric shawl with fancy stitches, a good way to get the feel for making a whole shawl or cape in crochet. Alison Schiff.

Multicolored Pinafores

One of Gloria Lynn's young friends liked her bright and lacy pinafore so much she wore it as a wedding dress, with a silk dress underneath the pinafore. The skirt is made with double crochets and filet mesh in subtle shades of blue, purple, and greens. The shape of the skirt is achieved by lots of increases from the waist down. The fullness at the bottom gives a lovely ruffled effect. The top is straight and unshaped and the button-back straps work like an old-fashioned apron. You will need to increase at least once every sixth stitch to achieve the proper fullness. For the ruffled bottom, go several times into each stitch.

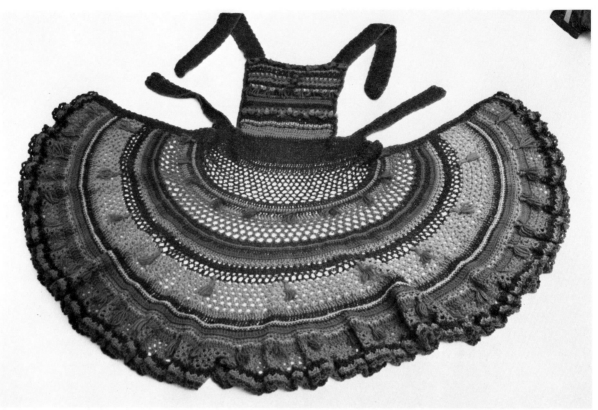

Fancy stitch tie-on pinafore. Gloria Lynn.

Fancy Stitch Sampler Vest

Vests are suitable for any age or sex. The illustrated vest is made entirely of straight pieces with no armhole shaping necessary. The sample is made in a monochromatic scheme of grays with black accents. It is an exercise in all the variations of the single crochet, shell stitch, popcorn, filet mesh, tapestry, and loop stitches.

To Make the Vest:

Make a chain that measures around your body just below the chest line. The chain should barely go around since the vest will be open.

Crochet two to four rows of all the stitches you want to practice until the piece reaches just above your hipline, about 5 or 6 inches for a person 5 foot 1 inch to 5 foot 6 inches tall. Change yarns to experiment with textures and colors as well as stitchery.

For the back, crochet a six-inch square of filet mesh. Slip-stitch this square to the center of the waistband. This is done with the two right sides facing each other.

Edge the 3 unattached sides of the filet square with a row of contrasting colored single crochets. Then add a border of 1 to 1½ inches on either side. The sample is bordered with a brick patterned tapestry stitch.

Six-inch-wide straps connect the vest at the front of the waist portion and the top of the backflap. The sample straps are done in cross-stitches with contrasting popcorns zipped in at intervals.

Edge the entire vest in single crochet. Don't forget to edge the inside armhole areas.

For a dashing finale, edge the bottom and inside edges and top of the backflap with loop stitches. These could be cut open for a fringed look.

Wearable sampler vest.

Rear view of wearable sampler vest. Eleven different stitches were used.

Crochet in the Round

6

Everything you have done so far has involved going back and forth in rows. You can also go around and around without turning your work and this opens up a whole new range of possibilities in terms of creating different shapes and forms.

Rounds are based on logical mathematical principles. The shape is started with a base circle that is increased with each round. Some crocheters start their circles with a base round of 4 stitches, which are increased to 8, 16, 24; others start with a base of 6 stitches, which are increased to 12, then to 24. The key number in all circles, no matter what their starting base, is 12, since all increases after 24 stitches are attained are made on the multiples-of-12 idea. Let's see exactly how a circle is worked.

To Make a Flat Round:

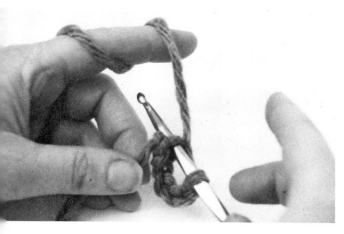

Chain 6 and slip-stitch the chain together.

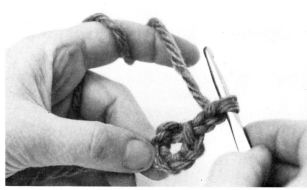

Chain 2. This is the first stitch of the round.

Make 11 double crochets into the center of the ring. This doubles your basic circle to 12 stitches. For the next round, chain up two again and make two stitches into every stitch, which will give you another 12 stitches, a total of 24 stitches. On the following round, increase every *other* stitch, to bring your stitch total to 36.

You can work your rounds in singles or doubles. Here is a single and a double crochet circle, both increased to the 36 stitch point. You can see how the use of short or tall stitches helps you control and determine the size of your shape.

Making Very Large Circles

Circles can grow well past the 36-stitch circumference, simply by continuing the 12-stitch increase pattern. After you reach the 36-stitch size, increase every 4th stitch so that you will attain 48 stitches; in the next round, increase every 5th stitch to gain another 12 stitches and a total of 60, and so forth. In order to keep the circle flat, increases made beyond the 36-stitch round should be made only every other row. Some crocheters don't count their increases at all, increasing at random whenever an increase seems needed.

Alternate Method of Selecting Your Round

The method of starting the circle with a chain and then crocheting twice the number of stitches into the center of the ring is probably the most frequently used one. We have another method passed onto us by a European aunt and one that we like particularly well since it gets us right into a base unit of 12 (or more) and still permits a tight center.

Here's how it works:

Start a slipknot as if to cast on a chain, but leave the slipknot loose.

Cast on stitches around the open slipknot.

When you have the desired basic circle, pull the loose string and tighten the center.

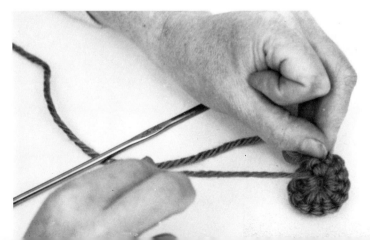

What Can You Do with Crocheted Rounds

To answer a question with a question, what can't you do with rounds? Rounds can be worked into stunning pillow covers, chair pads, room-sized rugs. Small rounds can be sewn together to make large blankets or clothing, or combined with other shapes, something you will learn more about in the next chapter.

The blending of colors and textures and using offbeat materials can give uniqueness to the simplest projects-in-the-round. Miss Joan Everett, a kindergarten teacher in Long Island, made over twenty mats from bread wrappers so that her students could sit on the floor during story hours. Her unusual mats could be adapted for outdoor chair pads, patio rugs, or beach mats.

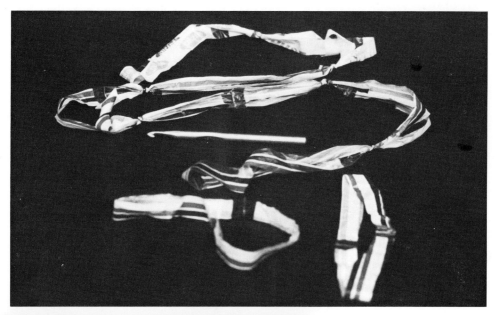

Bread wrappers are cut horizontally. The loops are knotted together to form the yarn. A J hook is used.

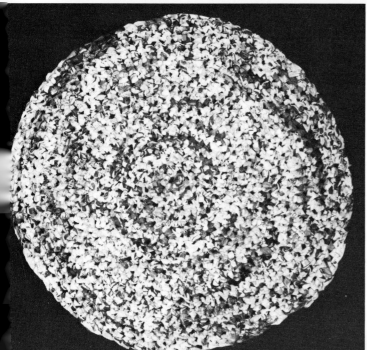

Bread wrapper mat. The colors of the plastic wrappers create an exciting tweed color scheme.

Learning to Be Free with Irregular
Spiraling Circles

By closing your circle rounds with a slip stitch and chaining up to start the next round you can always keep track of where each round begins. Sometimes, however, going round and round in an irregular spiraling pattern can produce a freer design pattern.

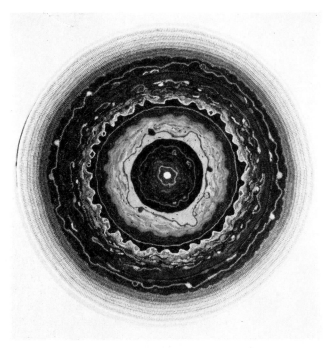

Variegated wool blanket. Renie Breskin Adams.

Detail of variegated wool blanket.

Cup-Shaped Rounds

If you keep increasing your circles, they will become bigger but remain flat. If you continue your rounds *without* increasing, the sides will start to fall down and your circle will turn into a cupped shape or bowl.

Since a hat is really an inverted bowl, your round is the perfect beginning for a crocheted hat, one of the all-time favorite crochet fashions. Hats can be easily custom fitted without any set pattern.

For a fitted cap, make a circle to fit the top, flat area of your head. A circle approximately 3½ inches in diameter fits the average head. Then stop increasing.

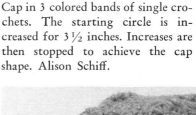

Cap in 3 colored bands of single crochets. The starting circle is increased for 3½ inches. Increases are then stopped to achieve the cap shape. Alison Schiff.

The basic cap shape dressed up with the use of shell stitches. Increases are made toward the bottom, so that the shells form a brim. Different colors are used for each row of shells.

Caps and berets call for a large flat circle, about the size of a plate. Once the desired fullness for the top of the hat is attained, decrease sharply until the hat fits snugly. The peak can be crocheted right to the edge of the hat. The illustrated cap was designed and crocheted by Gloria Lynn.

If you want your hat to have a flared brim, increase sharply. For a high crown, make a cap that extends beyond the shape of the head. The illustrated ruffled brim hat is made in thick red, white, and blue velour by Alison Schiff.

The basic cap can keep growing downward into a handy ski mask. The eyes and mouth are made like the buttonholes in the bag and belt projects (Chapter 3). Chain the desired number of stitches and skip the corresponding number of stitches and continue crocheting. Voilà . . . eye and mouth slits. Alison Schiff.

Embellishments for Hats

The fun and fantasy spirit in all of us has every chance for expression in the making of hats.

This hat with its multiple layers of ruffles was inspired by a Chinese pagoda. Though it looks complicated . . .

. . . it started with a plain cap. Rows of stitches were picked up from the surfaces. These raised rows were enlarged with increases stepped up each row to enlarge and fluff out the ruffles. A variety of textures and colors were used.

Bucky King likes to let all sorts of dangling parts grow out of her hats. She considers this one of her more "conservative" fantasies.

Gloria Lynn crocheted a whole series of pop art hats. The earrings were crocheted around a piece of bent wire in the same manner stitches were cast onto the large rings in Chapter 3.

Pompons and Fringes

Pompons and fringes can add important embellishing touches to things other than hats, but this is a good time to learn how to make them for hats or anything.

Pompons are nicest when they are full. Make yourself a template from a piece of cardboard . . . three or four inches or whatever length you wish. Wind yarn around the template about fifty times. Cut the ends open. Then take a longer piece of yarn and tie it securely at the center. Sew the pompon to your base, using the uncut thread you used to tie up your pompon.

Tie your pompon at the center. Don't cut the ends of the thread—you will use it to sew your pompon in place.

Boy's hat with a fluffy pompon and a simple tapestry design in orange and white wool.

To Make a Fringe

Fold yarn in half and loop through the edge as shown . . .

. . . pull tight.

With the aid of fringing, Gloria Lynn creates another pop art creation.

A double fringe accents the back of a beret hat. Gloria Lynn.

Crochet Pottery

As already stated, hats are really inverted bowls. Here we see Renie Breskin Adams exploring some bowl shapes with her crochet hook. The baskets and eggcups are soft but firm enough to stand without support. The eggs are stuffed. The whole concept of crochet pottery, boxes, and baskets will be explored in depth in Chapter 12.

Crocheted and stuffed eggs in eggcups. Renie Breskin Adams.

Crocheting in the Round over Hard Objects

A variety of objects can be made by using a pot or other hard object as an armature. The armature can be used inside the finished object or removed. If you work with a sturdy material such as twine, cord, or rug yarn, the object will retain its shape without the armature. It can be further stiffened by coating the interior with a glaze of half white glue and half water, which dries clear and hardly affects the texture.

An empty cheese crock was used as an armature for a covered box of white corde. Without the cover this would make a handsome planter.

The decorations of driftwood disks etched with a woodburning pencil were encased in metallic copper cord, illustrating yet another way to work around hard objects.

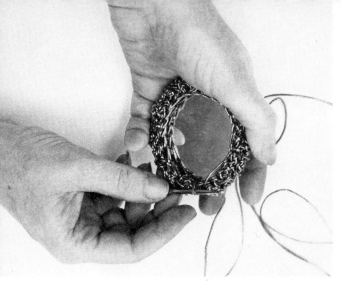

To firmly encase objects such as wooden buttons, mirrors, or stones, crochet a circle to fit the object, then decrease sharply, holding the object in place. Firm, nonstretchy materials are a must for this technique.

Gloria Lynn achieves the enclosed effect without hard objects. She makes small wool fringes and tufts the edges, then crochets around these.

Detail of soft enclosure technique.

Le Jeune Whitney crochets around bottles which she first paints to highlight the colors of her yarn. Both bottles are started with a basic round for the bottom of the bottle. The bottle at the left was worked with random, horizontal stitches, the one at the right in a vertical pattern. The circle was decreased and worked in tight singles for the neck. The neck covering extended beyond the bottle so it could be turned back to form a collar. Several rows of raised stitches are added to form ridges. Photo courtesy artist.

Forest Landscape jacket by Dina Schwartz. Photo by Mike Sommer.

Crochet-covered hassock. Houses and trees are stuffed and appliquéd. Figures have stone heads, clay bodies, and crocheted clothes. Elyse Sommer. Photo by Mike Sommer.

Three hats typifying the fun and fantasy potential of crocheted hats. Janet Lipkin. Courtesy artist.

Crocheted bird over welded steel armature, with Dacron stuffing and appliqué. 9′ x 9′ wingspan. Sharon Hedges. Photo by Mike Sommer.

Chrysanthemum and Daisy Planters. Elyse Sommer. Photo by Mike Sommer.

Free-form crochet worked into a 27″ steel ring. Ruth Walters. Courtesy artist.

Corde, wool, and bead collar necklace. Elyse Sommer. Photo by Mike Sommer.

Wool, velour, and bead necklace of organic shapes, some worked three-dimensionally. Elyse Sommer. Photo by Mike Sommer.

The colors for this scallop-edged cape were inspired by the fall scenery. Cloudlike mohair was used for the ruffled neckline. Elyse Sommer. Photo by Mike Sommer.

CROCHET WITH STITCHERY ON THE WALL. Renie Breskin Adams. Courtesy artist.

TO PRACTICE, REMEMBER TO PRACTICE TO REMEMBER. Sculptural crochet hanging, by Ronald H. Goodman, 6′ x 7′ x 5′. Courtesy artist.

RED HORSE AND RIDER. Mary Lou Higgins. Stuffed crocheted figures. Horse over aluminum armature. Photo by Edward Higgins.

A geometric patchwork design is the central motif of a sheepskin-lined man's coat by Jean Williams Cacicedo. Courtesy artist.

ST. CLAIR CATCHING A STAR. Vest by Laura Demme. The face, which is woven, was the starting point. Photo courtesy artist.

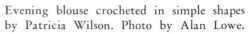
Evening blouse crocheted in simple shapes by Patricia Wilson. Photo by Alan Lowe.

Alpaca bag with appliquéd crochet shapes. Janet Lipkin. Courtesy artist.

Papier-Mâché-Crochet. Janet Lipkin. Courtesy artist.

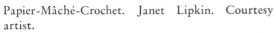

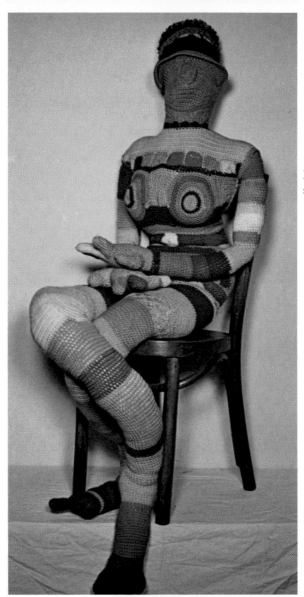

Life-sized stuffed sculpture. Patricia Wilson. Photo by Alan Lowe.

Chair sculpture by Shirley Saito. Photo courtesy artist.

Nesting mother and baby bird basket by Jean Williams Cacicedo. Photo courtesy artist.

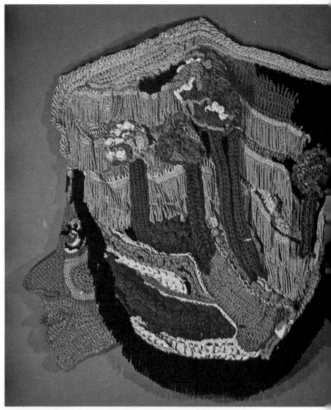

RAIN DREAMS. A crochet "painting" by Bonnie Meltzer. 40" x 50". Courtesy artist.

Patchwork crochet worked around a center of woven crocheted strips. Helen Bitar. Courtesy artist.

Another useful and attractive idea, a doorstop. A gray beach stone is encased with crocheted mohair and synthetic straw in shades of moss green. Le Jeune Whitney artist and photographer.

Arden Newsome, a well-known egg decorator, uses tapestry crochet worked in the round to encase real duck eggs. This technique is a good chance to recycle some of those handsome egg-shaped boxes in which panty hose are sold (L'Eggs).

Round into Square

Crochet rounds, in addition to turning into cupped shapes, can also turn into other flat shapes. The so-called granny square is actually made from a round base.

The easiest squares, the ones usually made into potholders as first projects by young children, are those where the stitches are worked back and forth in rows until the piece measures equally on all four sides. The square that grows out of a round core has a more sophisticated look.

Make a chain of four stitches and slip-stitch together. Chain 2 and make 7 stitches into the center of the ring. You now have a circle of 8 stitches.

On the next round, instead of increasing into each stitch all around, make three increases into *every other* stitch, which will form four corners.

In subsequent rounds, make three more increases into the middle stitch of the previous three increases, thus continuing the pattern of increasing at the corners. You will see these corner-increased stitches quite clearly as you work so that you'll be able to stop counting. You will note too that your increases are still based on the principle of 12 stitches per round increased.

Round-into-Square.

The Granny or Afghan Square

The traditional afghan square is also a square growing out of a round core. The only difference between this and the previously described round-into square is that the corners are worked with more increases so that they form clusters. Start as you did the regular round-into square, with a base chain of 8 stitches. From here on, the steps differ slightly:

Round 1: Chain 3 and make two double crochets into the same space as the chain. Chain 1 and make 3 more doubles, again into the same space. This is corner number one.

Chain 1, skip one space and make 3 doubles into one space. Chain one and make 3 more doubles again into the same space. This is corner number two. Corners 3 and 4 are repeats of corners 1 and 2.

Round 2: Use a new color and tie this into the center of one of the corner clusters. Do 3 doubles into the *space* (not the stitch). Chain 1 and do three more doubles into the same space. This completes your first corner. *Skip* the next three stitches and make your second corner as you made the first. Skip the next 3 stitches and make the third. Repeat for the 4th corner.

Round 3: Use still another color, and again tie in between the corner increase. Round 3 is a repeat of round 2 except that you will have two spaces in between the corners. Make 3 doubles into each of these. The squares can grow by following the procedure of round 3, always making an extra 3 doubles into the spaces in between the corners.

The Granny or Afghan Square.

Rounds into Hexagons

The easiest way to start the hexagon is to start your round with our alternate method of making 12 single crochets around a loose slipknot. Proceed exactly as you did for the square, making three increases into every other stitch. With a base of 12 stitches this will give you six increases and thus six corners. Continue your hexagon by making three increases into the middle of the increase of the previous rounds, thus maintaining your six corners

An octagon would work on the same principle. Here you will need a beginning circle of 16 stitches. Use the alternate method again, working 16 stitches around the open slipknot and increasing every other stitch or at eight corners. As you can see, this principle can be applied to any geometric shape.

Round-into-Hexagon.

Elongated Rounds . . . Ovals

Another useful and attractive shape is the oval. Unlike the regular round, the oval is built from a base chain. A row of singles are crocheted back along the chain as for back-and-forth work. However, once you get to the end of the first row, you keep going around the base chain. Here's how it works:

Cast on a chain as long as you want the inside of your oval to be. Crochet back along the chain. Make three stitches into the end stitch of the chain and work back along the other side. When you get to the end of the second side, make three stitches into the top stitch again and keep going around.

Keep enlarging your oval by making three stitches at each end. If your oval is to be a large one, do the increase in half doubles to emphasize the elongated shape. If you want your oval to be extra full, make an increase two stitches before and two stitches after the top increases. Ovals can be handsomely combined with other shapes. Two ovals stitched together at the sides and bottom make a handsome bag.

The Oval.

Half Ovals or Scallops

By doing only half an oval, very pretty scallop designs can grow out of a straight edge or even a central round. These scallops can be thin or fat.

To Make a Scallop:

Work a patch of single crochet stitches. Count to the halfway mark and chain up. The sample scallop is made by chaining up 9 stitches.

Single crochet back along the chain and complete the row.

To fill out the scallop, go back and forth. Skip a stitch at each side of the base, and do three stitches into the tip. The illustrated scallops show that your shapes can be thin or fat.

Three scallops worked off a straight-bottomed vest. The spacing was worked out with simple mathematics. The bottom of the vest had 60 stitches. The 60 stitches were divided into 4 to allow for two straight endpieces. Thus a scallop was made 3 times, every 15 stitches.

A Crocheted Clock with Rounds and Scallops

In addition to being a useful and attractive home accessory, the clock, with its twelve digits, serves to reemphasize the basic principle of increasing rounds in multiples of twelves. The digits are skinny scallops showing how these shapes can grow from a round as well as a straight edge. The process of filling in the spaces between the scalloped digits can be applied to any design that is worked from the center out rather than in the usual up and down manner. The clock was made with weaving wools, corde, and some acrylics. An old wooden plate into which a hole had been drilled was used as a backing for the clock, which could easily be used as the basis of a pillowcase or the motif for a vest or sweater.

A base round was increased to 60 stitches. The 60 stitches were divided by 12, which meant a scallop chain had to be made every 5 stitches all around. Each scallop was made with a chain of 10.

To fill in the triangular areas, pick up a stitch two stitches above the inside point . . .

. . . crochet down, skipping the point and . . .

. . . attach your stitch at the other side.

Single crochet into the other side and chain one to turn.

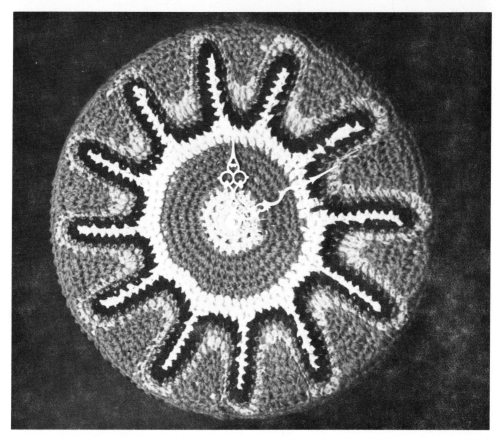

Here is the finished clock made with weaving wools, corde, and some acrylic. The clock cover was stretched over an old wooden plate into which a hole had been drilled for the clock part. Additional rows were made at the back of the clock, decreasing all around to firmly encase the clock. This is the same technique demonstrated for encasing smaller hard objects.

More Ideas for Projects in the Round: Handbags

A modern interpretation of a nineteenth-century tobacco bag. It starts with a circle that is gradually increased. Swedish wool and corde are used. After the row of popcorn stitches the bag is narrowed and 3 scallops are made to add shape interest. Beads are worked around the starting points of the scallops and also the bottom.

The tobacco bag that inspired the evening bag shown on the opposite page. It was made in 1880 by a Mrs. W. R. Alger of Boston. Photo courtesy Smithsonian Institution.

A large circle is squared out for this Cat's Face bag of yarn and fur by Mary Lou Higgins.

Patchwork Crochet

7

Since patchwork is a combination of lots of shapes into a whole, this chapter is in a sense a continuation of the last. Rounds, ovals, and hexagons are certainly all basic components of a possible patchwork design. In this chapter you will be rounding out your knowledge of shapes and how to combine them. Once you learn some additional geometrics as well as amorphous shapes you will have the wherewithal to figure out how to crochet any shape that comes to your mind.

The popularity of patchwork has brought with it the publication and exhibition of many traditional and modern patchwork designs. All of these are great potential idea sources for the crocheter. For more free-form types of designs you might go to another popular old craft, stained glass, for inspiration.

The simplest type of patchwork is of course that which combines lots of shapes of the same size into a whole unit. In recent years this type of patchwork has been applied to clothing as well as blankets and spreads.

A beautiful traditional patchwork afghan by Norma Getter. The granny squares are white, growing from a center rose motif.

The easiest square to make is one worked in straight rows. Delia Brock and Lorraine Bodger find small (2½-inch) squares have greater flexibility for clothing construction. The smaller squares tend to be more figure flattering too. This handsome boxy jacket required no shaping. Colorful squares are done in single crochets, edged with picots—a great way to use up leftover yarns.

The Triangle and Its Many Uses

Triangles are the basis of many patchwork designs. They can be added to hats to form earflaps.

Hat with two triangles crocheted at each side to act as earflaps. Gloria Lynn.

Large triangles can be sewn into a skirt recycled from a pair of pants.

Velvet pants recycled into a skirt by making a triangular insert of double crochets and shells. The flowers are crocheted in by crocheting a small circle to the surface and then increasing sharply all around, making 3 and 4 stitches into one until the flower shape emerges.

To Make a Triangle:

Starting at the point, chain 4.

Make a single crochet into the last chain of the base chain, chain 2, and turn.

Single crochet into the same space as the chain, single crochet into the next stitch, and make two singles into the last stitch—this completes a row of 4 stitches.

From now on make an increase at the beginning of each row.

For wider triangles, you may wish to increase at the beginning and end of a row. Triangles can also be started at the base and worked toward the point, in which case decreases are made.

Triangles into Diamonds

Diamonds are two triangles combined. Start your triangle at the point and, instead of ending off, continue on, reversing the increases to decreases until you get back to a point.

Patchwork Appliqués

Little triangles, diamonds, rounds, ovals, hexagons, and so on can be worked in a variety of yarns and sewn to clothing like appliqués. A number of shapes can be combined into a giant pop-art sort of appliqué as exemplified by the crocheted owl patch sewn to the back of a hooded sweatshirt.

This patchwork appliqué began with a fat oval to which two circles and a diamond nose are crocheted. The eyes are lightly stuffed with Dacron. Weaving wool and cotton are used.

Organic Patchwork Crochet

The most creative and, to our mind, the most fun, way to do patchwork crochet is to let one shape grow directly out of another.

The rear of the recycled velvet pants features a triangle that grows organically. The triangle begins with the diamond at the top and the other shapes are worked off that.

Let's take an organic patchwork pillow through its step-by-step development.

Five-Star Geometric Pillow

The design of this pillow grew from a central pentagon. This is bordered by 5 triangles and 5 quadrilateral triangles crocheted in between the triangles.

The numbers in the pattern indicate the progression of the crochet work. The dark, unnumbered triangles are optional additions showing how a design of this type can keep growing by the addition of more shapes.

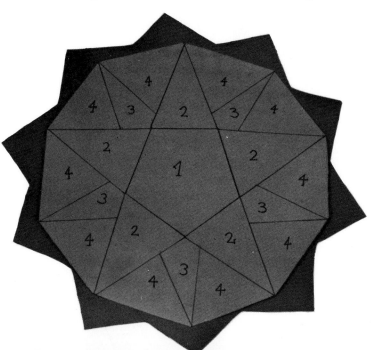

The three illustrated patterns are sized to combine into a pillow cover 15 inches in diameter. If you want to follow this pattern as a practice exercise, you can just hold your crocheting against these shapes to get the correct dimensions. No size pattern is needed for the number 4 triangle since it is filled in between the number 2 and 3 shapes and thus sizes itself.

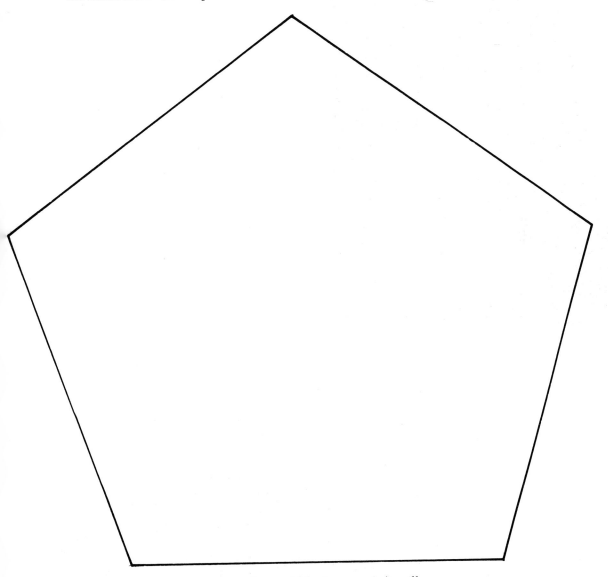

Pentagon pattern from which the rest of the pillow grows.

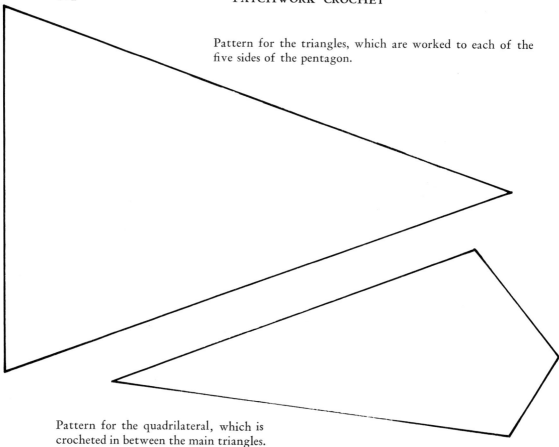

Pattern for the triangles, which are worked to each of the five sides of the pentagon.

Pattern for the quadrilateral, which is crocheted in between the main triangles.

To Make the Pentagon

Start your shape at the straight bottom and crochet just inside the line to allow for the contrasting yarn edging. Increase into the second stitch at the beginning of each row. When you get to the triangular portion decrease several times all across since this is a short section and the decreases must be made rapidly. Just keep holding the work against the pattern and you will be able to work out the exact number of decreases required. Write down what you do on the pattern in case you want to use it again.

To Make the Triangles

The triangles are cast right onto each side of the pentagon. Decrease into the second stitch of each row. The triangle is a tall one, so do several rows in the middle of the triangle without increases in order to get the proper height.

To Make the Quadrilateral

This is worked in between the triangles. Note that there is a long and short side and follow the placement of the overall pattern on page 100.

Attaching the Quadrilateral

Attach the quadrilateral 6 stitches above the base of the triangle and crochet across to the other side. Go up one extra stitch, and chain one to turn.

Work back across to the other side, attach the last stitch and again go up one extra, chain and turn.

To Complete the Pillow

The number 4 triangle of the basic pattern is attached in between the base triangle and the quadrilateral triangle, working back and forth as just illustrated.

A piece of felt, about an inch smaller than the crocheted pillow cover, is cut to match the pentagon shape. The felt is edged with a blanket stitch to which several rounds of single crochets are added. The front and back are crocheted together with a popcorn stitch edging. A stuffing of Dacron is inserted just before the edges are closed. Don't be stingy with your stuffing. The plumper the pillow, the nicer it looks.

The 5-star geometric pillow complete. White, blue, and gold wool is edged with dark brown wool and gold corde.

Hexagon Motifs for Patchwork

Hexagon motifs worked from a base round of 12 stitches with increases made at six corners (see last chapter, page 89) can be used for attractive patchwork designs. Another pillow illustrates how hexagons can be combined with other shapes.

Seven motifs are worked separately. Six are attached at each side, forming a circle. The six shapes are attached to the center hexagon with a single crochet worked on the right side to create a raised ridge. The points are accented with popcorn stitches worked into each corner. Once the basic shapes are attached, the pillow continues to grow organically.

The little diamonds growing out of the spaces between the pentagon are a variation of the fill-in technique used to attach the number 4 triangles in the five-star geometric pillow. Instead of working from side to side, starting at the base of the triangle, the attachment is made at the top point. You crochet from the top down to the base and back up to the top. Skip a stitch every time you get to the base and this automatically pushes up the shape to create a natural diamond.

To keep building on the hexagon base, large triangles are worked from diamond point to diamond point. The final edging again has popcorns at the six points. The back is again worked in felt, edged with a blanket stitch and several rows of single crochets.

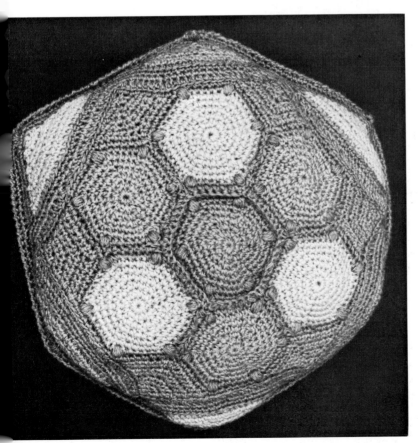

Hexagons, diamonds, and triangles in soft green, gold, and beige handspun, with blue used as an edging color throughout.

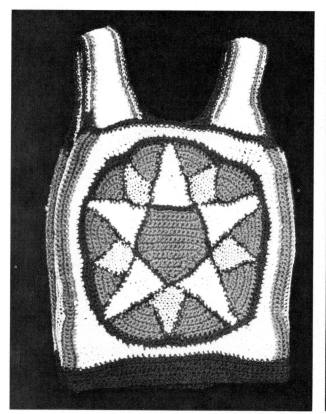

To show the versatility of the geometric patchwork, here is the 5-star pillow design used for a vest. Weaving wool, a curly novelty wool, and some shiny rayon ribbon are used.

The back of the vest is made with a variation of the pentagon. The central pentagon is enlarged and worked in a tapestry stitch with a heart motif.

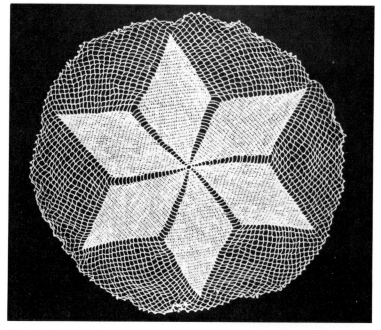

The inspiration inherent in geometric patchwork designs was not lost upon the old-fashioned dainty-doily makers. Collection Pearl Beck.

Here is a crochet interpretation of the star motif by Jean Williams Cacicedo. This striking man's coat is made of hand-spun wool, naturally dyed from sage and willow leaves. The collar is sheepskin. The coat won first prize in the Wyoming Golden Fleece and Spinning Competition. (See color section.)

Patricia Wilson used a 4-star motif for the front of an elegant evening vest crocheted in corde, macramé cord, and lurex yarn. Photo by Alan Lowe.

The back of Patricia Wilson's 4-star vest is a patchwork of circular shapes. (See color section.) Photo by Alan Lowe.

Using the Stained Glass Approach to Patchwork Design

In the stained glass method every shape of your patchwork can be different. Any large space can be broken up like a jigsaw puzzle. Each part of the jigsaw is then crocheted separately. The edging will be your "leading." This is a good exercise for learning to tackle all types of shapes. In the following pages are patterns for the shapes which comprise the sample stained glass design, with directions for crocheting the shapes. Follow the instructions as an exercise and then try to work out different approaches. Once you work these amorphous shapes, you will be able to tackle *any* shape.

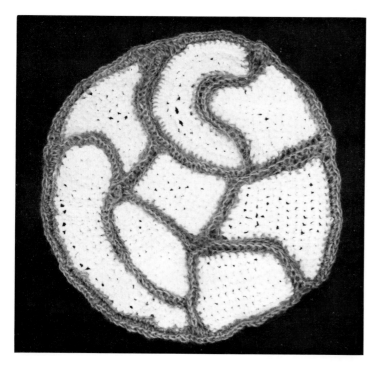

A circle is broken up into amorphous shapes, each of which is crocheted and then edged in a darker shade for a stained glass look.

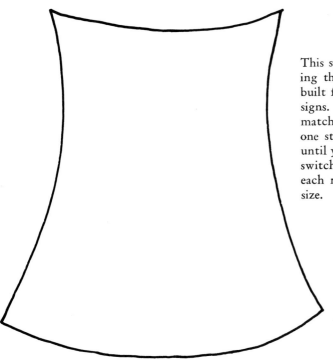

This spool shape can be varied by changing the dimensions. Other shapes can be built from it and it is found in many designs. Cast on a chain of stitches to match the wider bottom end and decrease one stitch at the beginning of each row until you get to the center. At that point, switch to increases at the beginning of each row until the spool has the desired size.

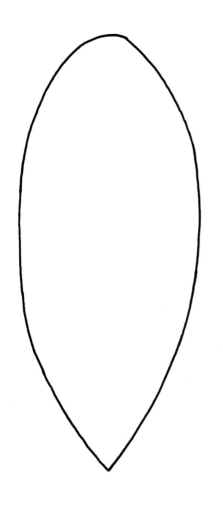

Leaflike shapes like this are essentially diamonds with rounded tops. Start at the triangle end by casting on 4 stitches. Single crochet into the last stitch and chain 2. Single crochet into the same space as the chain and single crochet into the next stitch, and do two singles into the last stitch (you've made 4 stitches). Chain one, turn and make an increase at the beginning of each row. When you get halfway up the leaf, make a decrease at the beginning. When you get to the top you should have 3 stitches left. To round off the leaf, do one single, one half double, one single and end off.

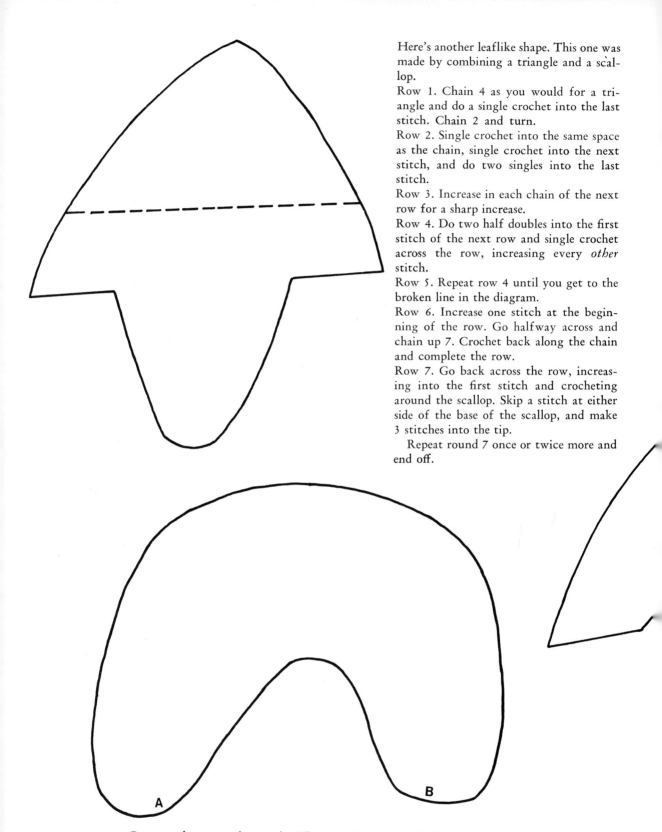

Here's another leaflike shape. This one was made by combining a triangle and a scallop.

Row 1. Chain 4 as you would for a triangle and do a single crochet into the last stitch. Chain 2 and turn.

Row 2. Single crochet into the same space as the chain, single crochet into the next stitch, and do two singles into the last stitch.

Row 3. Increase in each chain of the next row for a sharp increase.

Row 4. Do two half doubles into the first stitch of the next row and single crochet across the row, increasing every *other* stitch.

Row 5. Repeat row 4 until you get to the broken line in the diagram.

Row 6. Increase one stitch at the beginning of the row. Go halfway across and chain up 7. Crochet back along the chain and complete the row.

Row 7. Go back across the row, increasing into the first stitch and crocheting around the scallop. Skip a stitch at either side of the base of the scallop, and make 3 stitches into the tip.

Repeat round 7 once or twice more and end off.

Crescent shapes are fun to do. They can be made with both ends even, with long tails and short tails, skinny or fat. The sample was started at point A, along the inside curve. The procedure could be reversed, starting at the top; or, the crescent could be formed by going back and forth in short rows from one end to the other (see the banana shape that follows).

To make the crescent, cast on a chain long enough to reach from A to B in the diagram. Row 1. Do one single crochet into each of the first two stitches, two singles into each stitch until you get to the curve; 3 singles into each stitch until you get past the curve, and then one increase every other stitch until you finish the longer end. (An even-sided crescent would be done by repeating with two singles into every stitch once past the curve.)

Row 2. Go back along the first row, reversing the procedure. Decrease every other stitch until the curve; decrease three times throughout the curve, and twice until just before the ends. Repeat rows one and two, increasing on one side and decreasing going back, until your crescent has the desired fullness.

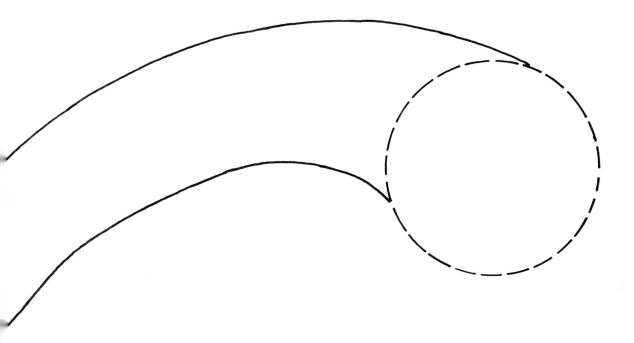

This banana-shaped form is really a stretched-out version of the crescent. The sample was started at the top with a circle. For the circle, chain 6, slip-stitch together and chain two. Do 11 double crochets into the circle and, on the next round, do two doubles into each space. Slip-stitch the circle together and start working downward in this manner:

Row 1: Do two singles, two half doubles, two doubles, and chain 3 to turn.

Row 2: Do one double, two half doubles, and two singles, and chain 1 to turn.

Rows 1 and 2 establish the pattern of stitches to be used all the way down.

Row 3: Now, to obtain the curve, decrease into the singles and continue the row with half doubles and doubles.

Round 4: Now increase once into each double and once into each half double. Do the single crochets without increasing.

Repeat rows 3 and 4 until you have the curve. Then continue in the singles-half doubles-doubles patterns without increasing or decreasing until you have the length you want.

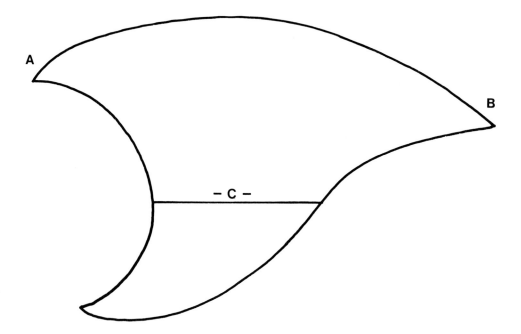

The bell is another exercise in increasing and decreasing sharply to achieve curves. The sample was started at the top.

Cast on a chain, which extends from A to B in the pattern. Begin decreasing as you work back along the chain, decreasing into every third stitch. Make another row of increases into every third stitch and then decrease once at the beginning of each row until you get to the line marked C in the diagram.

The pointed bottom is made by doing a row of 1 double crochet, two half doubles, and one single. When you go back along this row, decrease into the single and do one double into the first stitch of the last row.

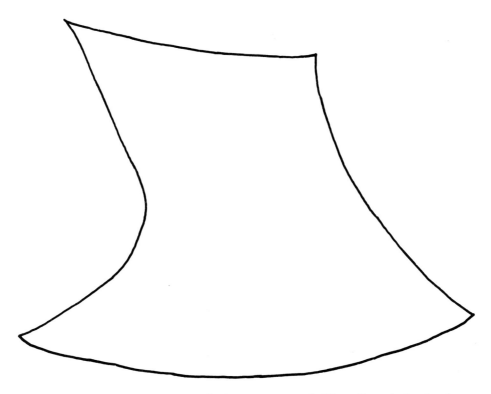

This odd-shaped spool can be made like the less pointy spool. Use taller stitches in the corners so that they will stand out more sharply. You could also work a less angled spool and then add little triangles at the corners.

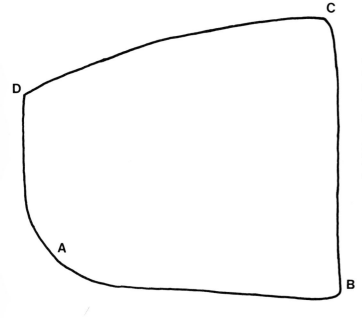

Amorphous shapes of all sorts can be easily followed by using increases and decreases and varying short stitches with taller ones. The sample was started with a chain reaching from A to B in the diagram. Half doubles are made into the A corner, singles on the B side. The last row is finished off with singles, half doubles, and doubles.

Patchwork Hangings

Shapes and stitch samples can be combined into lovely hangings like this 3′ by 4′ patchwork by Patricia Wilson. Note the use of open spaces and the clay beads made by youngsters at P.S. 179 in New York City. Photo by Alan Lowe.

Shapes grow out of an openwork central shape in a 3′ by 5′ hanging of gray and black wool, horsehair, and feathers. Artist, Mary Stephens Nelson; photo by Tom Henscheid. From the collection of Mr. and Mrs. S. Hatch Barrett.

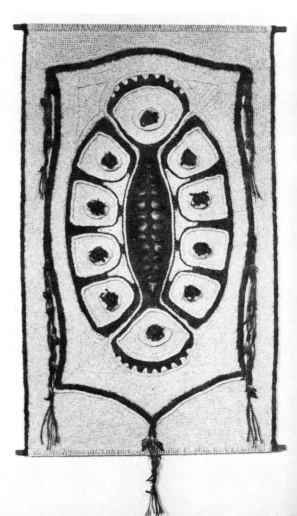

Crazy Quilt Patchwork

Helen Bitar works shape upon shape upon shape. Some she crochets together organically; others are sewn together later. In some instances, she adds additional colors and forms on top of her basic patchwork.

Every shape of this crazy quilt patchwork by Helen Bitar is different. Random rows connect circles and half rounds. Many stitches are used. Photo courtesy artist.

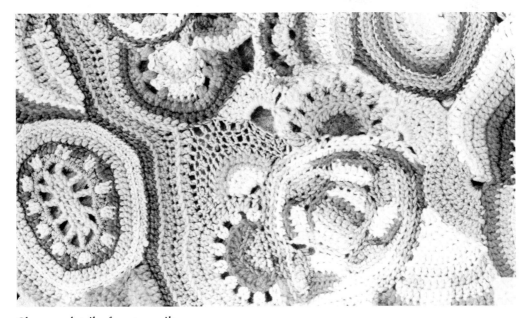

Close-up detail of crazy quilt.

Crazy quilt patchwork, with built-up dangles. Anyone using this as a bed blanket is likely to stay wide awake playing with all the dangles. Helen Bitar.

Close-up detail, patchwork plus dangles.

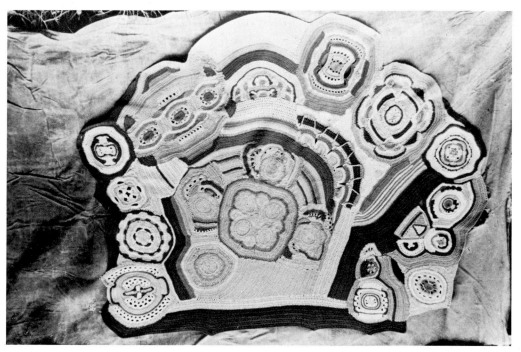

Another random crochet patchwork made while the artist was traveling cross-country. Purples and greens predominate. Helen Bitar.

Clothing

8

There is something almost irresistible about crocheted clothes and accessories. If you consider your body as an armature, the garments you crochet become not only one-of-a-kind trend-transcending fashions but sculptures. The very nature of crochet will help you gather courage to work without set patterns. Crochet stretches and gives so that fit is much more flexible than with other fabrics. The wide range of sewing patterns available can be utilized by the crocheter as a shortcut to patternmaking.

If crocheting a whole vest, sweater, or coat seems too ambitious a project for those of you who have never crocheted or sewn, why not gather courage with some small, basically nonfitted crocheted wearables. If you've worked through the various practice projects, you have already made several nonfitted vests (wearable sample vest, p. 73, halter p. 54). Let's start with some recycling ideas.

Recycling Old Clothes with Crochet Additions

No matter what the whims of fashion designers, you can adjust the hemline of a dress you like with crochet hems, which can grow if need be, or be partly ripped and re-edged if shorter skirts are in vogue.

Lorraine Bodger gave one of her favorite dresses not only a fashionably correct length but an entire new look with the addition of a multicolor hemline in single crochets and a tapestry stitch pattern.

To carry through the crocheted hem of her dress, Lorraine decided to add crochet sleeves. She used a filet stitch pattern, with a single crocheted cuff edged in picots. The armholes and dress closing are embroidered with single crochet chains stitched to the fabric.

To Crochet a Sleeve:

There are two ways of working sleeves.

1. Crochet the sleeve right into the armhole opening, casting on at the bottom of the armhole and going around and around. You can connect the circle with a slip stitch and work in a tube, or leave the tube unconnected and work back and forth. If you are working into a sewn material, attach your first row with a blanket stitch and then crochet off that. In order for the sleeve to conform to the upper arm, make some increases as you work along the outside of the arm and a few decreases where the sleeve will meet under the arm. After the first five or six rows you can work straight until you get below the elbow, when you decrease gradually to conform to the wrist.

2. The second method of crocheting sleeves is to use a sewing pattern sleeve as a guide. Crochet the sleeve to fit inside the dotted line. This eliminates the seam allowance needed when sewing fabrics but not necessary in crochet since crocheted garments stretch to a natural seam allowance. Sew or slip-stitch the rectangular portion of the sleeve into a tube and sew the curved portion from one side of the underarm, across the shoulder line and down along the other side of the underarm.

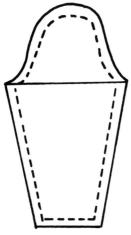

This is what a sewing pattern for a sleeve that is sewn around the armhole looks like.

Another dress partly in crochet. In this case, the crocheted collar and sleeves serve as textural contrast for Mary Lou Higgins's other skill as a weaver. The puffed effect of the sleeves is achieved quite simply by making lots of increases, then decreasing sharply.

Backless Tops to Fit Any Size

By updating the old-fashioned apron with its around-the-neck and around-the-waist straps, you can eliminate the whole problem of sizing and shaping. This has already been demonstrated in the pinafore dress by Gloria Lynn (page 72). Alison Schiff has worked this easy-fit concept into button-on halter tops, which have been sold through her crafts cooperative, Show of Hands.

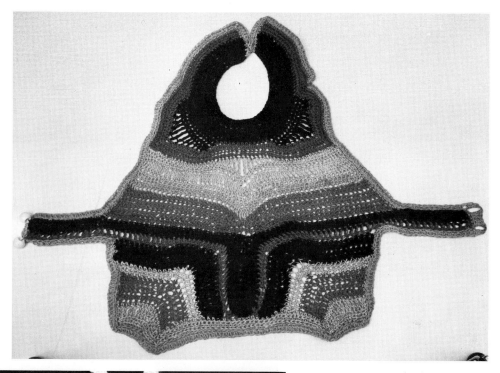

Button-on vest in red, black, orange, and rust cotton.

Another granny square halter. In this case an octagon square is made and the length is extended with a ruffle worked halfway down and around.

The button-on top made with a large granny square. Two button-back triangles are crocheted to each side of the hexagon and two **V** straps connect the neck.

Simple construction by no means limits you to simple designs. Here is a tieback halter worked in a brilliant patchwork of free-form shapes. Blue and purple predominate, with accents in white, green, and orange. Jean Williams Cacicedo. Courtesy artist.

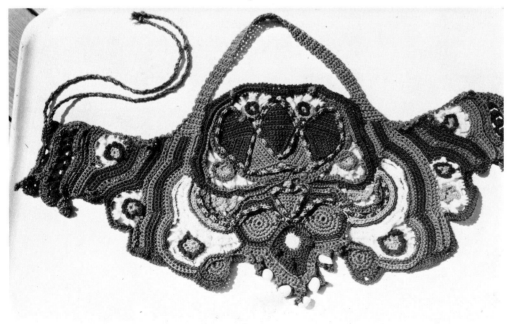

Capes and Shawls

Capes and shawls are fun and easy to make, practical to wear. It's best to start them at the top, casting on a chain to measure around the neckline, then working downward. Increases must be made all around to give the desired degree of fullness.

Nancy Clarke Hewitt's capes are convertible cape-skirts. She uses double crochets throughout with a corded edge at the hemline so that the garment holds its shape. Her colors are muted and sophisticated. Photo by Mary Kay Bernitt.

The narrow starting circle makes for a snug and flattering waistline.

Susan Lyttle went back to the top of the poncho to add on the hood and ruffles. Photo courtesy artist.

Rear view of Susan Lyttle's poncho.

Capes are a fine opportunity to practice fancy stitches, as exemplified by this cape by Patricia Wilson. (A landscape translated into a fancy stitch cape by Elyse Sommer can be seen in the color section.) Photo by Alan Lowe.

Diana Schmidt Willner's cape evokes visions of elegant evenings. Note the delightful "fur" neckpiece. Photo by Iris Schneider.

A shawl of lacy motifs and amorphous tapestry stitched shapes fitted inside a triangular frame with an extra crossband across the middle. Alison Schiff.

Self-Shaping Super-Easy-Fit Sweater

Designers Delia Brock and Lorraine Bodger have a knack for shortcuts that really work. Taking advantage of the stretch factor in crochet, they often don't bother at all with shaped armholes, simply going straight up and letting the finished item do its own stretching to conform to the body.

Their dashing little striped blouse is worked on the principle that the body is a tube. A chain is cast on, long enough to just barely fit from one side of the waist to the other. A straight rectangle is then worked, stopping only to change colors every few rows to create the stripes. The rectangle, or open tube, is worked all the way up to where the shoulder begins. Then the little shoulder pieces are worked separately on each side. The back is a replica of the front. The sweater is sewn together at the shoulders and laced with a crochet chain at the open side, which makes for an adjustable waist. The sleeves, like the body, are straight tubes and can be crocheted right into the open armhole.

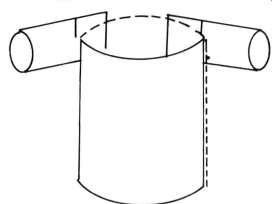

Sketch showing how sweater can be worked like a rectangle fitting around the body. Sleeves are also pieces shaped into tubes. Neckpieces are done separately.

Super-easy-fit striped sweater. Lorraine Bodger and Delia Brock.

Dressmaking Patterns

Why do you need a pattern, you may ask, if you can follow the simple process just illustrated?

Working with patterns enables you to create in many directions and will give an even more custom-fitted look to what you make. By using a pattern you can use the patchwork approach of letting shapes grow onto each other, starting at the center, as well as top or bottom. Let's start with the pattern and then see how a design is developed to fit the pattern.

The popularity of sewing has brought with it the publication of patterns in all sizes and shapes. Patterns developed especially for knits are ideal for crocheting. There are some things that need to be done to these sewing patterns to give them maximum crochet utility.

Since patterns come in half pieces, it's best to make up the other half so that you have the entire back and the entire front before you. The easiest procedure is this: Combine the front half into a full front by tracing it onto large sheets of newsprint paper. If you can't get plain newsprint, use large double sheets of a paper such as the *New York Times*. Cut out a dozen of these since they will be your scrap patterns for sketching out your crochet designs.

Cut out one pattern on a tracing pattern fabric or interfacing, available in all fabric stores. This will be sturdier than the paper for trying against your body. It can be used again and again for other things you crochet.

In other words, you are cutting a sample paper pattern on which you can scribble out your design ideas, and also a more permanent pattern out of a cheap pattern cloth to use for fitting. Making the cloth pattern is an optional step.

As already stated in the description for sleeve making, you can ignore the dotted line on patterns, which is for seam allowance and not necessary in crochet, which stretches.

Making Your Own Pattern

Following are the steps for making a basic pattern that can be used for a blouse, vest, or jacket. If lengthened, it can become a dress. Once you understand how a pattern is made to fit body dimensions you won't even need the sewing patterns, and if you do use them, you will be better able to make adjustments as you need and want them.

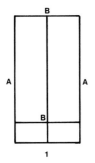
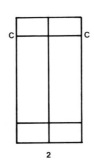

Diagrams for making your own pattern: sketches 1, 2, 3, 4, 5, 6.

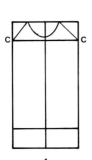
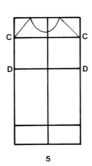
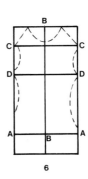
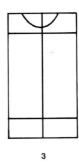

Step One

Hold a tape measure around your body, reaching across your bust. Divide this measure in half. This is the width of the base of your pattern . . . from A-A in sketch 1.

Step Two

Measure from the base of your neck to wherever you want your pattern to go (hip, hem length?). This becomes the length of your pattern . . . line B-B in sketch 1.

Step Three

Draw a line 3 inches below the top of the base pattern . . . line C-C, sketch 2.

Step Four

Now take a 7-inch plate and use it as a template to draw a circle between lines B and C, sketch 3. This is the neckline.

Step Five

Draw a line from each neck edge to the edge of line C, sketch 4. This is your shoulder line.

Step Six

Measure the distance from the top of your shoulder to the center of the bust and draw a line the length of this below the C-C line . . . D-D, in sketch 5. This is the length of the armhole (usually about 8 inches). Mark a curve from C to D for the curve of the armhole.

Step Seven

For a well-shaped garment, mark a slight curve between lines D and A so that the garment will nip in at the waist and go out at the hips. See sketch 6.

Make a paper pattern for sketching out your ideas and one cloth pattern that you can keep as a fitting pattern, as suggested for the ready-made patterns.

Crocheting a Vest to Fit a Paper Pattern

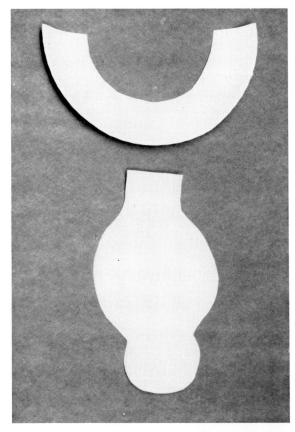

The vest began with a doodle plus a collar shape. The original plan was to make a bib necklace.

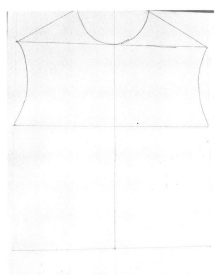

A basic blouse pattern is transferred to a piece of newsprint paper.

The pattern is adjusted for the vest, which will have deep armholes and closings at the front and back collar.

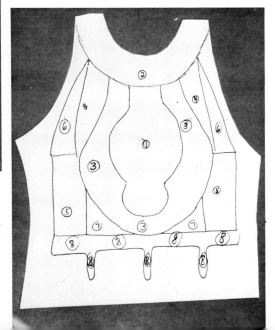

The pattern is laid out in terms of shapes to be used.

Here's how each part of the vest was worked out in terms of yarn and color. Single crochets were used throughout. The ridge stitch was used for all the velour sections. The descriptive numbers correspond with the numbers in the pattern diagram on page 129.

1. The doodle was started at the straight top with gradual increases as it ballooned out. To emphasize the wide areas, half double crochets were used for the increases in the middle section. Gold corde was edged with light blue wool.

2. The collar was also crocheted in gold and blue. A chain was made to fit the inside collar line and increases were made all across, immediately. There was an increase every third stitch, every other row, but this could vary according to the yarn used.

3. The collar and doodle were slip-stitched together and the central shape enlarged by edging all around in light blue wool, deep blue velour, and yellow rayon ribbon. To keep the form from buckling, increases were made at all the curved areas as needed.

4. Long velour triangles were picked up at the collar and worked back and forth, always attached at the side of the central shape.

5. Another rectangular panel of velour was worked off the lower portion of the central shape. The last four rows are left unattached, creating two V's.

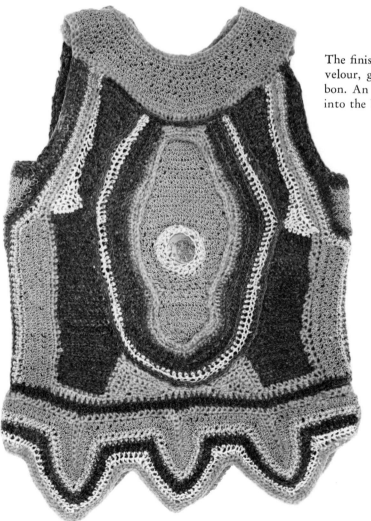

The finished vest in blue wools and velour, gold corde, and yellow ribbon. An extra triangle was worked into the bottom of each armhole.

6. Another triangle was worked between shapes 4 and 5 to again fill out the pattern shape—this time in yellow ribbon.

7. The V shapes were filled in with light blue wool. This straightened out the bottom edge of the vest.

8. The scalloped bottom began with a row of single crochets worked straight across. The stitches were divided into 4 parts. There were 60 stitches and so a chain of 9 was worked up and back every 15 stitches, three times. The scallops were rounded out with two rows each of the various yarns used. One row of hard light blue plastic ribbon was worked in to tie in with the last decorative touch of encasing a decoupage wooden button (a mirror, stone, or other decorative object could be used) in the plastic ribbon (see Chapter 6 for details of working around hard objects). The back of the vest matches the front.

The front and back collar pieces of the vest were closed with three crotcheted loops on either side of the front collar and 3 buttons on either side of the back collar.

Another scallop-edged vest. This time the edge is made with three large circles. Red, deep blue, and beige are accented with white wool. Patricia Wilson. Photo by Alan Lowe.

Free-form shapes in beiges and browns combine into a vest by Diana Schmidt Willner. Photo courtesy artist.

Rear view of free-form shape vest.

A Jacket of Geometric Shapes Fitted to a Paper Pattern

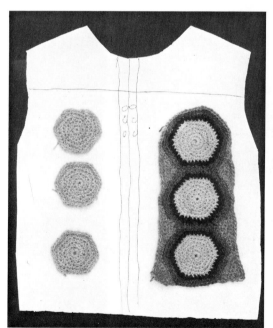

The basic pattern with the developing shapes. The hexagons are edged in contrasting yarns. Triangles were crocheted in between the connected shapes to fill out the forms.

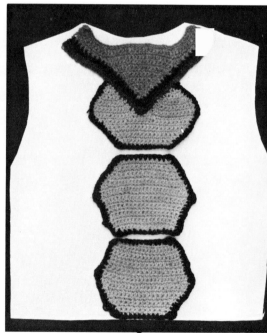

The hexagon pattern was carried out for the back. The top shape is crocheted right into the shoulder.

Front view of hexagon jacket. Mexican handspun and hand-dyed wool is used. The hexagons are pink and the accent colors blue and green. Beige and gray are used for the sleeve and large background areas to mute the brighter colors. The sleeves are crocheted right into the armhole, worked in a tube, with a few bands of popcorn stitches. The lower arm is finished in a tapestry pattern with triangles added at the wrist.

Two extra hexagons were attached on top of the bottom ones to serve as pockets. Note the popcorn stitches used throughout to emphasize the corners. The buttons are beads into which holes were drilled.

The collar is made as a straight band of stripes that stands up in back and falls into V shapes in front.

A jacket worked in solid pieces with 3-D crochet used to add decorative details. Patricia Wilson. Photo by Alan Lowe.

Free-Form Designing on a Dressmaking Form

For those making a lot of clothes, the dressmaker's form offers still more flexibility for free-form designing. Shapes can be pinned in place, then moved around before a final decision about what will be permanently attached is made. Dina Schwartz gave us an opportunity to photograph her as she did her first pinning on a coat. Though Dina works spontaneously, without detailed plan, she does usually make rough sketches and knows the general effect she wants, in this case, a wearable forest landscape.

134

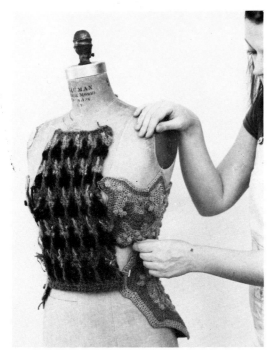

A side closing is planned to allow for a rich two-tone front panel. Amorphous shapes will make up the side panels. Open areas can be crocheted in once the major pieces are attached.

The second side is pinned in place.

A group of shapes crocheted around leather are pinned in place for the shoulder and upper arm.

The yarns of the front panel are repeated for the tree-shaped back panel.

135

More leather and wool "clouds" are pinned in place.

A lot of ruffled leaf shapes were made to form a collar.

Dina now has an idea of how her back will look.

She pins the lower part of her sleeve in place.

About two weeks after we photographed the pinning of the coat, Dina posed for us in the finished jacket. As you can see not everything remained exactly as originally pinned. The beautiful flowers were crocheted right into the front panel with lots of ruffling. (See color section.)

Rear view of Dina's forest coat.

Dina's technique of letting ruffled flowers grow out of her design was also used in this pinafore dress made for and modeled by her daughter Astra. The idea for the dress started with the tapestry landscape.

More Design Inspirations for Jackets and Vests

Diana Schmidt Willner, like Dina Schwartz, loves the combination of landscapes and crocheted clothing.

Landscape vest worked out against a paper pattern.

The front of the vest being laid out.

The finished vest in muted browns, gold, and off-white.

Another landscape coat, this one inspired by a Van Gogh painting titled *The Blossoming Chestnut Trees*. The front of the coat is crocheted in pieces, to resemble a cascade of blossoms.

The tree was the starting point for the back of the coat. Both hood and cuffs are lined with a silver gray sheepskin fur. The coat is lined with a melton wool that is appliquéd with a bare chestnut tree and blossoms on the ground.

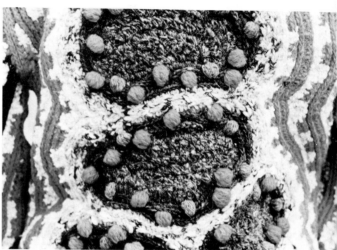

Janet Lipkin combines free-form shapes into a sweater reminiscent of a stained glass design. The amorphous shapes are gray, edged with red puff stitches and white accents. Photo courtesy artist.

Close-up detail of Janet Lipkin's winter sweater.

This vest with its rich contrast of pink, red, and white yarns in thin and thick textures became the inspiration for a second somewhat similar design for a coat. Laura Demme.

Rear view of vest.

Rear view of Christmas coat.

Norma Minkowitz combines knitting, crochet, and trapunto in an unusual vest of white and off-white cotton thread. Kobler/Dyer Studios.

Here is the coat inspired by the vest. It's in red, white, and black. The back panel and parts of the sleeves are worked in a tapestry stitch. Laura Demme calls this her Christmas coat.

Arlene Stimmel used arrows as her central motif for a vest sparked with mirrors.

141

For those who wonder if there is a market for offbeat and intricate crochet clothing, here is a photo of a window display at Julie's Artisan Gallery featuring clothes by Arlene Stimmel, Sharon Hedges, and Dina Schwartz. Clothing galleries like this do attract buyers who not only appreciate but are willing to pay the right prices for this type of work-manship. Photo by Iris Schneider.

Portrait Designs

Laura Demme launched her art career as a full-time weaver, then fell in love with the look and flexibility of crochet. She still uses her weaving skills in combination with crochet as proved by her very unique vest, which started with a woven face and grew into a figure, complete with halo and tree.

In the tradition of the true craftsman, Laura gives as much care to a lining as to the outside of her garments. Here is the St. Clair vest beautifully lined in double knit wool with embroidery and appliquéd shapes.

St. Clair Catching a Star Vest. Laura Demme. (See color section.) Photo by Iris Schneider.

Diana Schmidt Willner's portrait coat was inspired by some cut paper collages by Matisse. The portrait is crocheted.

Front view of the portrait coat.

Side view of the portrait coat.

Crochet Clothes That Never Require Closet Space

Many crocheters think of the garments they crochet as three-dimensional sculptural body ornaments and eventually plan their designs with the additional function of wall or floor/table ornament in mind.

Margaret Ballantyne's technique consists of a simple single crochet stitch. However, she uses her yarn to create forms with great flow. Photo courtesy artist.

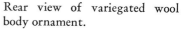

Rear view of variegated wool body ornament.

Since the artist manipulates her yarn so that it is quite firm, her body ornament works equally well as a three-dimensional sculpture, independent of the body armature.

Laura Demme created this vest she calls MIRROR MAN (the title stems from her fascination with cartoon characters) so that it can also be hung as a wall hanging when not worn.

Rear view of MIRROR MAN vest.

Buttons at the side enable the owner to open the vest and show it off as a wall hanging.

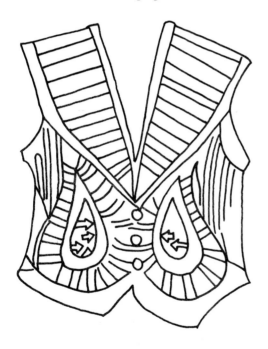

Here are copies of Laura's original sketches of the vest. She colors her sketches with crayons so she can visualize the yarn and colors as well as her shapes.

Accessories

Hats, the most popular of all crochet accessories have already been covered quite fully in Chapter 6, since they are most commonly worked in the round. Not all hats are made in the round, however. Some artists use rectangles and squares. Laura Demme's unusual California hat started with a rectangle

CALIFORNIA HAT. Laura Demme.
Photo courtesy artist.

crocheted in a tapestry stitch pattern. Shells were crocheted on top of the rectangle, giving a padded effect. The peak was stuffed to hold its shape. The hanging shape was made by sewing together two triangles and stuffing them.

Handbags

Any two shapes can be sewn together to make a handbag. Handbags can also be made in the round (illustrations page 95). Handbags also afford another opportunity for fantasy interpretations like Janet Lipkin's bone bag inspired by the shape of dog biscuits, and Diana Willner's Hearts bag.

Janet Lipkin's bone bag is crocheted in wool and alpaca, which, when finished, was brushed with a wire dog brush. The shapes are crochet appliquéd, and the inside of the bag is lined with hand-painted muslin. (See color section.)

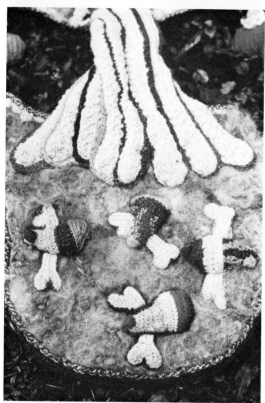

Close-up view of bone bag. Note how the shapes are holding the dog bones.

Another crocheted and appliquéd bag, this one by Diana Schmidt Willner. The large heart was crocheted separately, stuffed and crocheted to the front panel of the bag.

Rear view of Diana Schmidt Willner's Bag of Hearts. The handle is lined and the inside lining quilted around hearts so that the inside reflects the outside forms.

Mittens

Mittens can be crocheted in two separate pieces or in a one-piece tube. The following demonstrations show mittens made with the two techniques. The two-piece mittens began with a diamond design at the center, with pieces built onto that organically. The tubular mittens began at the wrist, and the design was crocheted to the top of the mitten three-dimensionally.

To make mittens in two pieces, outline your hand on a piece of paper and follow the shape as you crochet along. The sample was started with a diamond that grows in different colors and textures. The wrist is started with triangles into which another shape will be crocheted.

The top and palm of the hand are crocheted together, skipping 5 or 6 stitches for the thumb tube.

Mittens can also be made all in one piece. A chain is made to fit around the wrist. This is slip-stitched together and the mitten is worked as a tube. Again stitches must be skipped to allow for the thumb.

Whichever way the mitten is constructed, the thumb is made by picking up stitches around the thumbhole, slip-stitching them together and working in a tube.

Both mittens completed. The design for the all-in-one tubular mitten is created with raised single crochets.

Boots

Boots, like mittens, can be worked in two parts or on the tubular principle.

These handsome, leather-soled boots by Nicki Hitz Edson were photographed by Iris Schneider at Julie's Artisan Gallery.

Pet Accessories

Once you have made a pair of mittens or boots in the round or tubular technique, why not a touch of distinction for the furry friend in your life? Cast on a chain to measure around his body and work up toward the neck, making holes for the front paws. The rear paws will of course remain free to allow for his attendance to the true purpose of his walks.

Our miniature Schnauzer positively preens with pride every time he wears his tricolored coat with its pineapple stitch accents. It's made in stretchy acrylic yarn for easy on-and-off.

Jewelry

9

Crocheted neck and arm pieces are very much a part of the increasingly important soft jewelry scene. Like clothing, this is a form of portable art. The techniques and design methods presented in other chapters can be applied on a small, quick-to-finish scale.

Patchwork Necklaces

Small shapes can be combined in many wearable ways. Vary your yarn as the jeweler varies his metals.

Soft gold chenille laced with black threads is worked into small flat rounds. The circles are sharply decreased, as if to encase an object, thus double-layering the circle and giving it a three-dimensional look. Each disk is edged with picots, in black mohair. The neckband is a chain of the two yarns intertwined. Old gold beads are used as spacers and as a closing.

Crocheting Around Neckbands and Rings

The technique of crocheting around rings demonstrated in Chapter 3 can be applied to necklaces.

You can crochet around wire neckbands available from jewelry suppliers.

Begin an organic patchwork necklace by casting on stitches around a wire neckband. Two triangles begin the design.

The space between the triangle was filled by working from the top points of each triangle so that a diamond is formed. Other shapes and silver beads were crocheted on. The two ruffled shapes toward the bottom were worked separately. Weaving wool in earth colors is used, with wine red velour for the ruffles. (See color section.)

You can fashion your own neckbands from 18-gauge silver or brass wire.

Cut your wire to the desired length and use a form as a mandrel to bend your shape.

Use pliers to twist the ends into loops, leaving one end open to act as a closing hook.

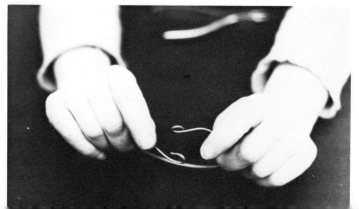

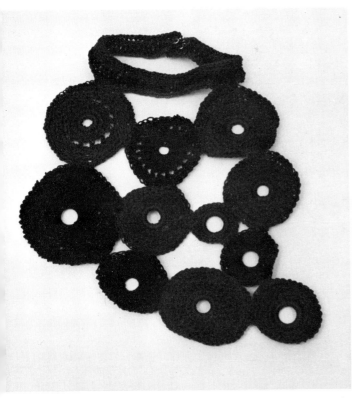

Alison Schiff crochets around plastic rings from the variety store and sews her crocheted rings into a big necklace. Try mixing colors, arranging different patterns.

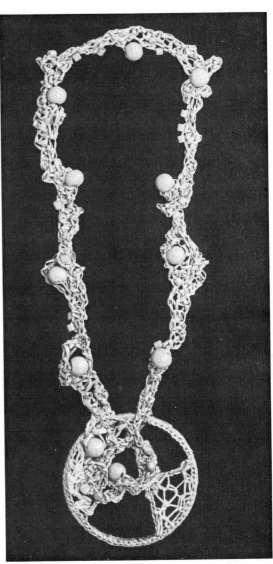

Le Jeune Whitney incorporates small mirrors into her free-form crocheted ring pendant.

Dorothy Hall's pendant necklace of synthetic rayon yarn and beads is a miniature version of the large freeform crochet designs into rings shown in Chapter 3.

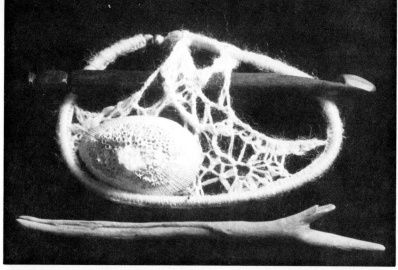

Hair ornament with shell. Dorothy Hall.

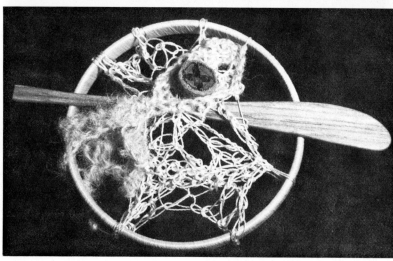

Another hair ornament, this one in hot pink and orange. Dorothy Hall.

Crocheted Gold

Jewelry crocheted in gold lamé thread may not be as valuable as the real thing, but it can be every bit as beautiful. Metallic yarns are available in silver, bronze-toned browns, and ruby reds. The yarn is thin and best worked on a thin steel hook. Simple stitches—single and double crochets—look best. The gold lamé can also be used as an elegant edge for a piece crocheted in heavier fibers.

Lamé thread is available in a variety of metallic shades, besides gold. A #1 steel hook works well with this type of thread. Shown here, a handsome wrist bracelet worked in a tight single crochet by Bucky King.

Gold Plus Beads

Beads add glamoúr and weight to lamé as well as other crocheted jewelry.

Antique gold beads are encased in gold lamé jacket. The beads are covered by making cupped rounds, as for a hat. The smaller beads are strung onto crochet chains. Bucky King.

When we spotted these dainty examples of Oaxacan green pottery at the famous Saturday market, we knew they had to become beads for a necklace.

Mary Lou Higgins creates a variety of cupped shapes. Clear beads are caged into chains of lamé. The forms combine into a flowing and graceful necklace.

Gold Wire

Fine-gauge brass or silver wire can be crocheted with interesting results.

We prefer a plastic hook when working with wire. Instead of starting the chain with a slipknot, simply twist the wire into a loop. From this point, the technique is the same as all crochet.

Unlike softer yarns, crocheted wire can be pulled and twisted to emphasize shape and form.

Gold brass collar necklace with cut sheet brass dangles. Pearl Beck.

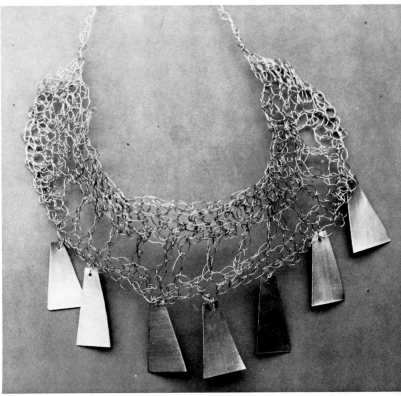

Gold Corde

Gold corde has the look of antiqued metal. It combines handsomely with wool, velour, and beads. The neckline of the neckpiece illustrated on the next page is started exactly like the lamé necklace with the pottery beads. A row of filet mesh was worked between rows of single crochets. Little scallops were worked off the last row of single crochets and then filled out with beads, wool, velour, and more beads. A corded edge is worked around the entire necklace. The filet pattern is worked through as a closing.

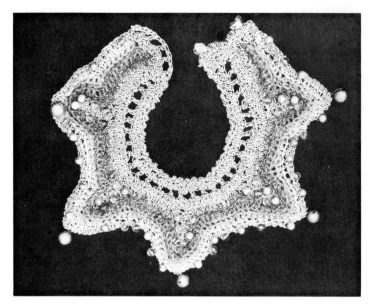

Gold corde, wool, and bead collar necklace. (See color section.)

Here is the collar necklace done in red and magenta wools and mohair. Dolly Curtis. Photo by Jack Curtis.

Copper and Plastic

The inventive jeweler is always on the lookout for new materials and combinations of materials. Here beads are made from casting resin, poured into small plastic ice-cube trays. The yarn for the neckband and bead cages is stiff copper cord, the sort of novelty material often found in bargain bins of yarn shops.

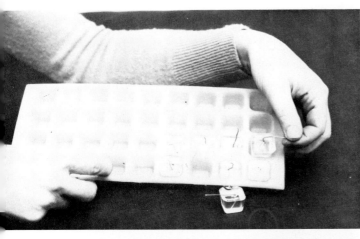

Bits of wire are inserted into the resin before it hardens. This makes it possible to lift the hardened cubes right out and . . .

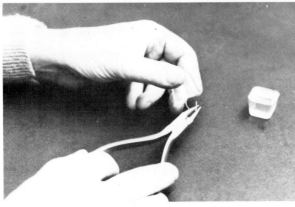

. . . twist the ends into a loop around which the crochet chains can be tightened.

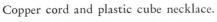

Copper cord and plastic cube necklace.

Crocheted Pearls

This pearl necklace by Renie Breskin Adams is 100 percent fiber. The pearls are stuffed. Some knotting is used for the stringing element and macramé for the knot.

Adjustable Body Ornaments

Jean Boardman Knorr's necklaces and arm ornaments remind us of mazes. The artist builds a whole network of loops and knots into her designs, making it possible to create a number of necklaces from one by means of adjusting the knots and loops. The wearer thus becomes a participant in the design as she searches out yet another way to wear the ornament.

Necklace of pink cotton. Jean Boardman Knorr.

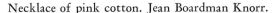

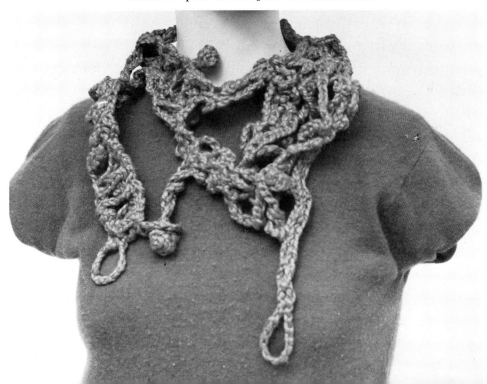

A variation of the same necklace.

Arm ornament in beige cotton and beads, also adjustable to different positions.

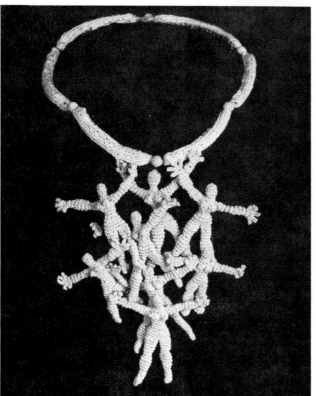

The sculptural possibilities of crochet ornaments are beautifully illustrated in this wool and cowhair design by Margaret Ballantyne. Photo courtesy artist.

Another sculptural necklace. Two-inch crochet figures form a bib for a neckband of knit-encased plastic tubes. Norma Minkowitz. Photo by Kobler/Dyer Studios.

Feathers can be crocheted right in place like beads or sewn on after. Feather and bead bib necklace. Alison Schiff.

A marriage of two richly textured materials, wool and lynx fur. Mary Lou Higgins. Photo by Edward Higgins.

Cotton cord and stoneware beads combine into a striking, primitive body ornament. Alison Schiff.

Mixed Media

10

Crochet is compatible with numerous other crafts and materials. Let's look at some mixed media ideas and methods.

Stitchery and Embroidery

The use of embroidery stitches to detail designs on a crocheted surface is a natural. You can make crochet chains and stitch them to the base, curling and shaping them as you go along. Some examples of this were given in Chapter 3, when the crochet chain was taught. You can also embroider by single crocheting a design onto the surface of your base fabric. Regular embroidery stitches can be made over and under the ridges of the crochet stitches.

This panel was inspired by a visit to the ruins of Mitla near Oaxaca, Mexico. The stones were picked up at the site of the pyramids and the crocheted panel stretched over a piece of wood. Raised single crochets in fine cotton were used to reinterpret some of the scrolls. The faces are drawn with India ink. The stones are glued to the crochet panel with a thick white glue.

Renie Breskin Adams uses a variety of embroidery stitches to "paint" her breakfast STILL LIFE onto a crochet panel.

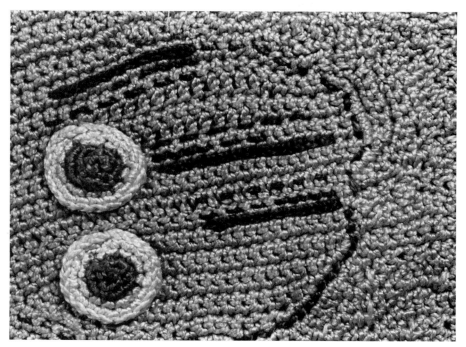

Close-up detail of STILL LIFE embroidery panel.

Another close-up detail of STILL LIFE embroidery panel.

Those who enjoy cross-stitch embroidery will find the afghan or Tunisian crochet stitch ideal since it forms a pattern much like a canvas for easy counting of stitches. This type of crochet closely resembles a knit texture and is worked with a special needle. Since it is most useful for stitchery we have not included instructions for it earlier.

How to Make the Basic Afghan Stitch

A special afghan hook that is as long as a knitting needle but hooked at the end is needed. These are available in all yarn supply stores. Start with a chain of the desired length, but when working back along the chain keep all the stitches on the needle. In other words, insert your hook into the chain, yarn over the hook, and draw through the loop; go onto the next stitch instead of working off the loops. *Do Not Turn.* Tunisian crochet is worked on one side only!

To work back along the first row . . .

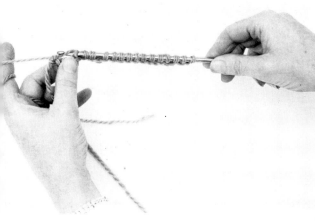

To work back along the base chain yarn over the hook and draw a loop through the first stitch on the hook. Next yarn over and draw through the next two loops and keep repeating this until only one loop is left.

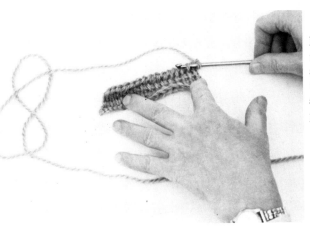

For the next row insert the hook under the vertical stitch from right to left as shown. Yarn over and draw the yarn through the loop and again keep all the stitches on the hook. This makes the box pattern.

Tunisian crochet squares are crocheted together with an arch stitch edge. The colorful cross-stitch embroidery motifs are effective against the black background. Lillian Grossman, artist. Collection of the authors.

Detail Tunisian crochet afghan and embroidery.

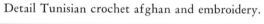

Dolly Curtis uses afghan square panels as a background for French knot and popcorn embroidery stitches, sparkled with the addition of seed beads and small mirrors. Photo courtesy artist.

Detail of mirror-bead and embroidery on afghan stitch panel.

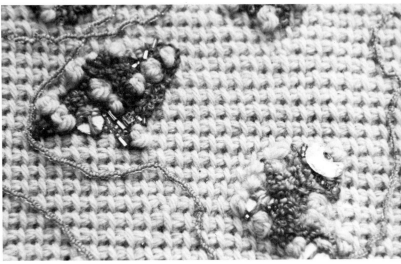

Wool and silk cross-stitch embroidery on a red and green table cover, made in the second half of the nineteenth century. Photo courtesy Smithsonian Institution.

Madge Copeland stretches free-form crochet shapes into a box frame. Some padding and stitchery are used. Courtesy artist.

Another box construction with crochet accents. Ahuvah Bebe Dushey.

Knitting, Padding, and Crochet

The combination of knitting and crocheting gives additional textural contrast to designs.

Knitting combines with crochet in SANDY'S PATCHWORK by Patricia Wilson. 3′ by 5′. Photo by Alan Lowe.

FACES AND FIGURES. Stuffed knitting and crochet table sculpture. 8″ x 14″. Norma Minkowitz. Photo by Kobler/ Dyer Studios.

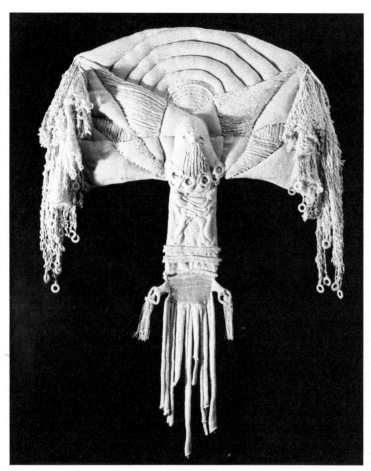

Knitting, padding, and crochet are combined in a 30″ x 44″ hanging by Norma Minkowitz. Notice the very modern look of the old-fashioned crochet-covered rings. Photo by Kobler/Dyer Studios.

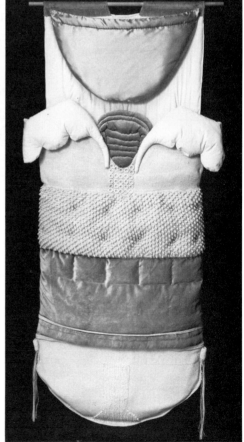

Sleeping Bag Wall Hanging, combining crochet, knitting, and trapunto. 33″ by 80″. Norma Minkowitz. Photo by Little Bobby Hanson.

Weaving and Crochet

Many weavers have become fascinated with the flexibility that crochet can lend to their work. Laura Demme's beautiful vest started with a woven portrait and developed with the addition of crochet. There are many other ways in which weaving can be combined with crochet.

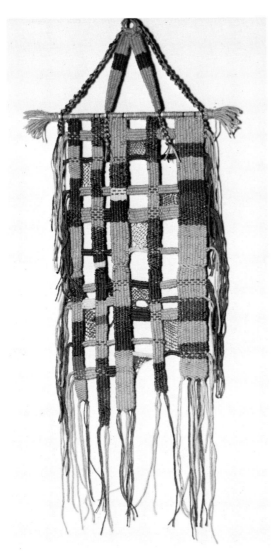

Bucky King adds tiny crochet panels to a woven hanging. Courtesy artist.

A black and white woven panel bought in a handicraft gallery is embellished with an edging of bright red crochet and small black pottery beads.

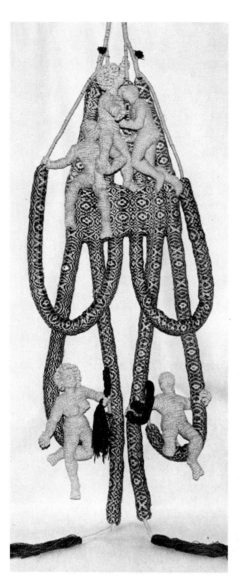

Mary Lou Higgins adds crocheted figures to her woven, stuffed hanging, TRYING TO FIND ONE'S OWN NICHE. Photo by Edward Higgins.

FACE AND FIGURES. Norma Minkowitz. Weaving with crochet appliqué and embroidery. 28″ by 48″. Photo by Kobler/Dyer Studios. Collection Julius Gold.

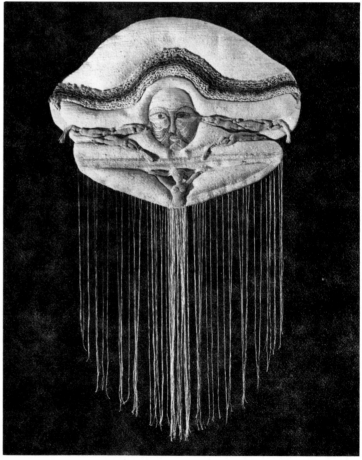

Clay and Crochet

Ruth Walters, a potter who became fascinated with crochet, used some of her crocheted forms as a means of achieving an exciting surface for her pottery.

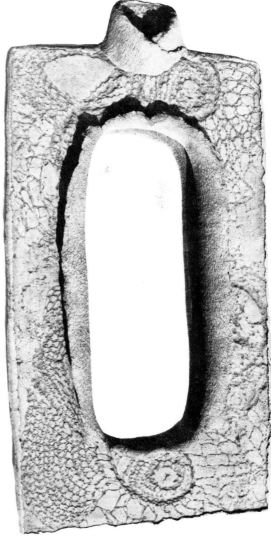

Weed holders illustrating two methods of texturing clay with crochet. At left, the crochet is pressed into the surface. At right, a reverse design is made by means of impressing crochet into a flat slab, firing the slab to bisque hardness and then using this slab as an impression mold. Ruth Walters. Photo courtesy artist.

Stoneware mirror with crochet fabric impression. 12″ x 22″. Ruth Walters. Courtesy artist.

Leather and Crochet

Leather and crochet seem to almost belong together. Stitches can be worked off any fabric either by sewing on the crochet work or making blanket stitches along the edge and working single crochets off the blanket stitches. When adding crochet to leather, the process is even simpler. Punch holes along edge with a leather hole punch and work your stitches right into the holes. Use a #1 steel hook for your first row so you can keep your holes small and close together.

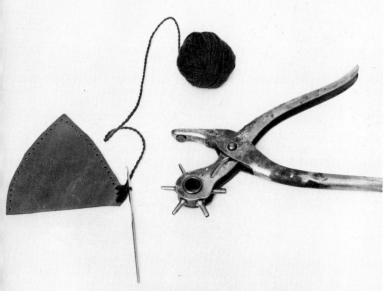

Leather holed so stitches can be made into leather.

Blue, orange, and yellow wool mittens with tan leather palms.

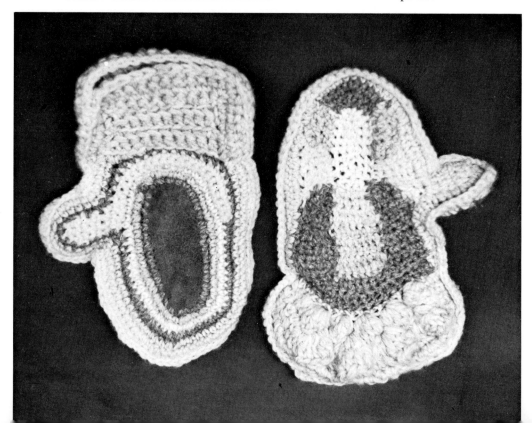

A beige leather crown and peak are combined with thick brown
and gold handspun wool and beige bouclé.

Leather bottoms make crocheted boots and slippers much more wearable.
Alison Schiff.

A bag worked in the round, off a circular leather bottom with leather insets. Alison Schiff.

Leather patchwork vest. Alison Schiff.

A bag of mostly leather. The inset is done in a tapestry stitch. The sides are crocheted. The handles are worked with triple stranded yarn for extra strength.

Miscellaneous

Mixed media ideas don't always happen all at once. Mike Sommer's clay musician sat on a shelf happily "bare" for almost a year. Then a trip to Mexico suggested the idea for creating an environment for the sculpture. A piece of leather, somewhat smaller than the sculpture base, was holed, and a single crochet base for a grass garden was added, decreasing at the edge so that the clay and crochet work would be firmly of one piece. The grass grew with loop stitches of soft green velour, and little ruffled flowers of novelty yarns grew right out of the grass. A tapestry-stitched rebozo and big-brimmed hat completed the picture.

Leather bottom with crochet starts environment for clay sculpture.

MARIACHI PLAYER IN A GARDEN. Sculpture Mike Sommer; crochet Elyse Sommer.

Mary Lou Higgins makes her own ceramic molds and holes the edges so the crochet can be stitched into the mold, as with crochet and leather. MOTHER NATURE. Photo by Edward Higgins.

Papier-mâché is another ceramic-like base for crochet. Janet Lipkin made her construction over a chicken wire armature. The feet are made with instant papier-mâché. The underside of the wings are painted and shellacked. The crochet is sewn right through the papier-mâché form. The beak is movable. (See color section for another view). Photo courtesy artist.

Rug Craft and Crochet

Long before ecology became a household word, economy-minded housewives learned to recycle scraps to fashion floor coverings. Along with hooking and braiding techniques they used shirring, which was done by gathering together ¾- to 1-inch bias strips of fabric and sewing them from the center out into circular mats.

Louise McCrady has improved upon this fine old craft by combining rug craft with crocheting. She calls her method Shirret, pronounced *shu-ray*, to rhyme with crochet. She uses a special needle (see supply sources) which, like the Tunisian crochet hook, is longer and also has a special fingerhold indentation that keeps the hook in working position and frees the thumb and forefinger for pushing the folds. The cut fabric strips do not need to be sewn together. The needle is woven in and out of the strips until it is filled. The folds are then attached with a double crochet stitch made with a cotton warp thread in between each fold. As each stitch is completed, a fold of fabric is slipped off the needle. The crochet stitches form a web of warp through the folds of the fabric, giving it great strength. Since the crochet warp is hidden, the rug is completely reversible. The ¾-inch thickness gives it a plush texture and makes it feel almost as if foam rubber were hidden within the fabric. In the following photo series Louise demonstrates her techniques.

The fabric is cut into strips that are threaded onto the shirret needle by running the hook in and out through the center of each strip.

The needle is designed with a special fingerhold to keep the hook in working position. Louise illustrates the best way to hold the needle. The hook should always point downward.

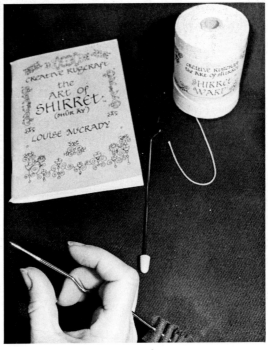

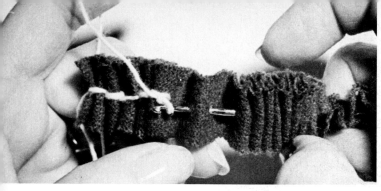

The crochet work starts with a chain stitch row. Each chain stitch of warp is pulled through a fold as the fold is slipped off the needle.

Crochet continues on the opposite side of the chain stitch row with double crochet stitches worked through the warp strands, between the folds.

After each double crochet, the fold is pulled off the needle, thus each row of folds is interlocked between folds of the preceding row. The structural stitches form a web of warp that is strong and durable.

Pieces can be made any shape or size as shown in this picture of Louise at work on an oval rug in process, surrounded by some of her other rugs.

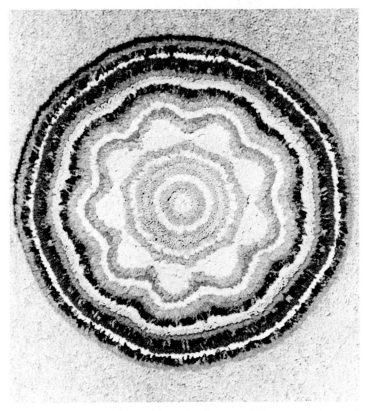

Fifteen-inch round chair pad made of many different weights and textures of wool.

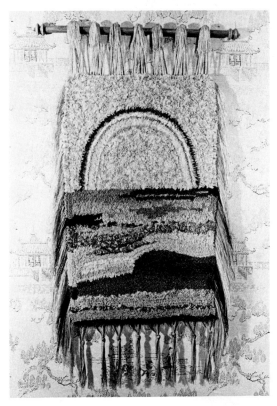

Shirret hanging, GEOLOGY I, 18" x 36", made of many different cottons.

Sculpture

11

The reader who has been progressing through this book, experimenting with techniques and ideas, has already created sculptural forms. Since anything three-dimensional falls into the category of soft sculpture it was impossible to contain all crochet sculpture within this one chapter.

A hat is a three-dimensional form. Clothing, as already stated in Chapter 8, can be considered a form of sculpture with the body as an armature. When you make mittens in a tube you are using the same technique you would use to make a figure.

Let's take one more type of sculpture not usually thought of in that sense and then see how artists, working with large-scale sculptural forms, apply the same basic technique to their work.

Puppets and Toys

All puppets start from a tube made by casting on a chain long enough to fit around the puppeteer's arm. The chain is slip-stitched together to form a circle. Two stitches are chained up to begin the first round. At the end of each round the tube is slip-stitched together, the stitches again chained up. There are no increases for the portion of the puppet that fits the puppeteer's arm.

To shape the head, increases are made at intervals all around. The amount of fullness wanted determines the pattern of increases. To narrow the head, decreases are made. A second tube for the lower part of the puppet's mouth and the puppeteer's finger is needed. This is added by first leaving a hole in the desired spot. This is done like a buttonhole: Chain up the desired number of stitches for the opening and skip the corresponding number of chains before resuming your crocheting. When the top tube is finished, stitches are picked up around the hole and another tube of the desired length and width is worked.

Alison Schiff created a whole menagerie of puppets for her two children, all worked on a tubular principle.

Snake.

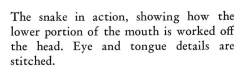

The snake in action, showing how the lower portion of the mouth is worked off the head. Eye and tongue details are stitched.

A not very ferocious lion.

This mouse was modeled after the Schiff family's own pet mouse. The ears are added separately, each made up of two triangles stitched together and lightly stuffed.

An elephant like this offers good practice in sharply increasing and decreasing a tube. The pink ears are separate shapes stitched onto the tube.

The rabbit's ears are again separate, lightly stuffed pieces.

Stuffed Toys

Stuffed toys are a great way to give vent to your imagination while you get your feet wet as a soft sculptor.

Stuffed toy in red, white, and blue. Dina Schwartz.

Stuffed fantasy beast of many shapes and stitches. Dina Schwartz.

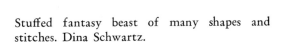

Astra Schwartz has not only a mother to crochet toys for her but friends. This whimsical bird made for Astra when she was a baby by designer Janet Lipkin still hangs in her room today.

For those who favor miniatures, these tiny crocheted toys were brought back from a trip to Japan by Dee Weber.

Sculptural Samplers

We've seen sampler hangings and wearable samplers. Here, Patricia Wilson demonstrates that samplers can be made as stuffed and sculptural forms.

Stuffed sampler hanging. Patricia Wilson. Photo by Alan Lowe.

Another abstract stuffed form worked with a sampling of fancy stitches and embellishments. Patricia Wilson. See color section for a more realistic sculptural form by this artist. Photo by Alan Lowe.

Masks

Nicki Edson's masks are sculptural flights of fancy. Masks can be worked like hats, starting at the crown and then adding embellishments to the base shape. Nicki starts hers with the part of the mask that intrigues her the most. In the case of her animal masks, this is always the nose. The Czar Mask, on the next page, began with the towers.

Dragon Mask in red wool with green trim. The mouth and tongue are wired; eyebrows, teeth, and nose are stuffed. Nicki Hitz Edson.

Czar Mask in tweed wools, plain wools, edged
with gold metallic. The face is separate and snaps
on or off the hat. The towers, rocks, nose, and
beard are stuffed. Nicki Hitz Edson.

Soft Sculptures Based on Human Forms

Making a human figure in crochet is an extension of the puppet-making
technique. Arms, legs, and bosoms must be provided. Increases and decreases
must be planned to nip in waists, round out heads, and so on. If you work in
stiff fibers your form can be self-supporting. Most soft sculptors use stuffing.
When working on a large scale, there is also the possibility of working over an
armature.

Your figure can start anywhere. Mary Lou Higgins starts her figures from
the head, which is essentially a hat that is continued on, narrowed down toward
the neck. We like to start our forms at the hip, working up toward the head
and then adding legs later on.

Figure started at the hips. The tube is narrowed with all-around decreases for the waist, widened for the torso. Holes are left at the front for crocheting in a bosom for a female figure and, a row above this, holes are left for the arms. The bosom could also be appliquéd over a solid torso.

Stitches are picked up around the bottom of the torso with a chain of stitches that are slip-stitched together for the start of the thigh-tube.

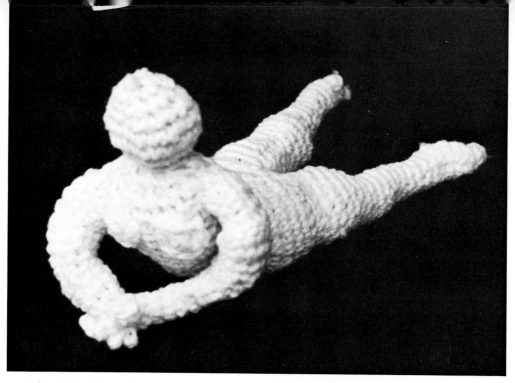

The finished form is stuffed making it firm but flexible. Fingers can be made with picots.

Using Crocheted Figures to Make Artistic Statements

Mary Lou Higgins combines groups of her beautiful forms into unusual sculptural hangings. She uses both stuffing and aluminum armatures to support her sculptures as you will see in the following step-by-step demonstration. This animal and human sculpture is part of a series the artist calls Yahoo. The illustrated sculpture stands 2½ feet tall. A single crochet stitch and G hook are used throughout. Another of the artist's horse and rider sculptures can be seen in the color section. The photos are by Edward Higgins.

An aluminum frame is shaped into an armature. Interlocking sections are taped together with heavy-duty plastic tape.

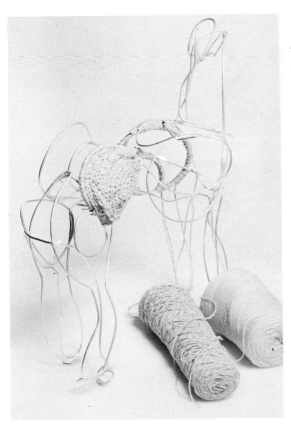

Two colors of wool are crocheted onto the armature.

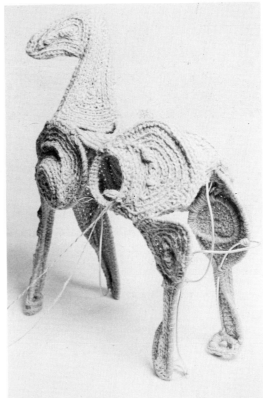

Crocheted sections are gradually filled from the frame toward the center.

Tail and mane are tied into the crocheted areas.

A card-woven horse blanket trimmed with Egyptian paste beads is added.

A male rider that will be stuffed with polyester fill is begun, starting with the head.

The torso is finished and the thigh begun.

When the legs are complete, the arms are begun.

The figure, complete with fingers, is positioned onto the horse.

The female figure is begun.

The two figures are sewn in place and beads are added for a bridle and around the horse's tail.

YAHOO, completed.

Profile view of YAHOO.

Rear view of YAHOO.

Life-sized Figures

Bonnie Meltzer began crocheting in life-sized proportions when she created a series of costumes for a children's play. One of her latest sculptures represents her reflections upon the bad and the beautiful in today's world. Her ANTI-BURGLARY LADY is constructed to fit nicely on a window ledge and resembles a window sitter—with everything that this connotes. She is a hard brassy lady with rings and red nail polish, shiny red hair. Fringe, braids, ribbons, as well as traditional yarns, are used and both stuffing and an armature support the form.

The inside of the lady's head presents the contrasts in the world around us for it lifts up to reveal an interior scene of green grass, a romping dog, and a bright blue sky with puffy white clouds. See the color section for a life-sized sculpture by Patricia Wilson.

ANTI-BURGLARY LADY, life-sized. Bonnie Meltzer. Photo courtesy artist.

Abstract Sculptural Forms

Jane Knight's reputation as an outstanding sculptor in crochet is well deserved. Her forms, whether stuffed or supported with wire rings, have a purity and rhythm that is sheer poetry. Richard Knight has photographed some of Jane's ring-supported sculptures as well as one of her stuffed hangings in its developmental stages so that the reader can get a clear picture of the artist's methods.

An 8-foot sculptural hanging of rug wool with wire rings supporting top and bottom shapes.

Detail.

Detail.

Another ring-supported hanging with tubular forms growing out of the main sections. 4½ feet.

Detail.

Jane's hangings are crocheted with nylon, when intended for outdoor use since wool would eventually rot if exposed to the elements.

The Development of a Stuffed Sculpture

Heavy rug wool is crocheted with thick wooden hook inherited by the artist from her grandmother, and probably close to a hundred years old.

The basic form is folded and stuffed with polyester fill.

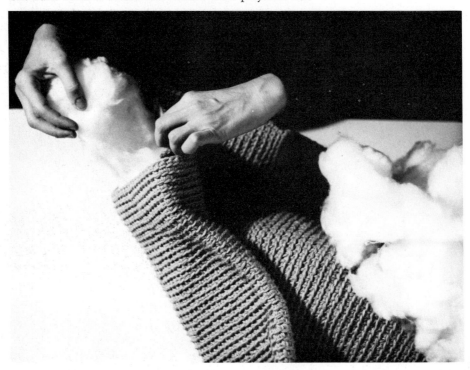

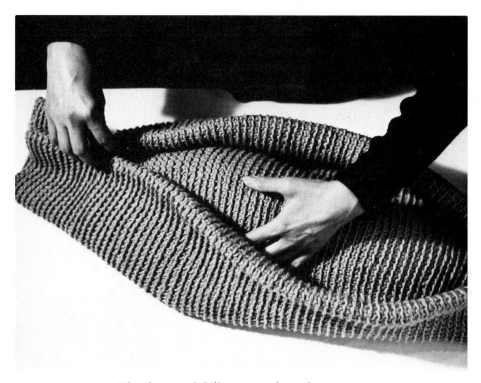

The shape and fullness are adjusted.

Dangling forms are added by crocheting back along a base chain with lots of increases. These will be filled into the open area of the hanging.

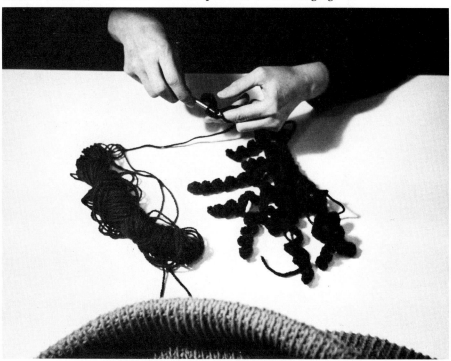

The finished piece. It measures 4 feet.

Many sculptural hangings evoke a sense of mystery and mysticism, yet the basic forms are actually reminiscent of more functional things like hats.

Susan Lyttle blends many colors, yarns, and stitches into a form she calls Evolution III.

Detail of Evolution III.

Detail of Evolution III.

Inspiration for crochet sculpture comes from many sources. Judy Manley's companion sculptures, TOUCHSTONES: ME and TOUCHSTONES: YOU, were visualized when she read *Open Marriage*. She wanted to interpret the authors' statements about each person being a many-faceted human being, with each facet serving as a hookup for making contact with others. The body of each piece is a stuffed tube, with lots of holes left so that small tubes or touch points could be crocheted on. Handspun cotton from Haiti was used for the body with some handspun wool for the touch points.

TOUCHPOINTS—ME, 18″ x 70″.

TOUCHPOINTS—YOU, 28″ x 70″.

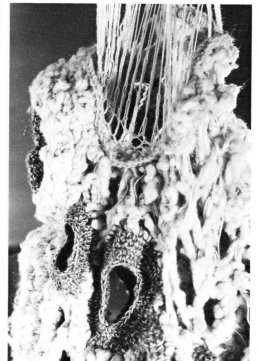

Detail of MEDUSA.

MEDUSA: GIFT FROM THE SEA was Judy Manley's first all-crocheted thing. Many fibers worked almost exclusively in single crochets were used, with some soft plastic coated picture wire crocheted on some spots to make the piece hold its shape.

THE LADY is a small floor sculpture representing Judy's further experimentation with fibers. The figure is crocheted from the center of a 10-pound cone of natural jute and around a central core of pandanus branch some of which can be seen sticking out from above the lady's eyes.

Helen Webster's fascination with nature and the sea is reflected in much of her work. She believes that lots of preplanning in no way prevents spontaneity. She makes sketches, determines exact dimensions, and thoroughly thinks through her pieces before she begins. According to Helen, "the delightful accident or surprise will *still* happen."

JACK-IN-THE-PULPIT. 56". Another well-planned-out sculpture grew out of a series of slides taken of a patch of jack-in-the-pulpits from spring shoots to fall berries. The stem and covering hood of jute are crocheted around an old lamp base to which stuffing was added to take away the hardness.

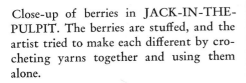

Close-up of berries in JACK-IN-THE-PULPIT. The berries are stuffed, and the artist tried to make each different by crocheting yarns together and using them alone.

Helen Webster's love of the sea plus an article on cooking squid served as a launching point for a wrapped and crocheted sculpture, aptly titled GIANT SQUID. Jute of different weights and thicknesses was single crocheted. The wrapping was added to give body and structure. The twists in the tentacles were made by increasing on one side of the tube and decreasing on the other, and moving the increase and decrease areas in a regular progression each time around.

Wool, rayon, and chenille, all in off-white tones, are used to create a hanging. Photo by Tom Henscheid. Collection of Mr. and Mrs. Richard J. Sanders.

Mary Stephens Nelson often finds unusual materials a starting point for her explorations with the three-dimensional.

Details of off-white hanging.

Plastic agricultural twine that is very stiff and makes for a very strong structure was built into a 26″ form Mary Stephens Nelson calls FEVER TREE.

Flexible Crochet

We'd like to conclude this chapter with a sculptural concept we consider especially noteworthy in an era often associated with the word alienation.

Margaret Ballantyne's sculptures are made up of pieces that can be taken apart and put together in many ways. This actively involves the viewer in the constant changes in the form that never ends. The artist is fascinated with embellishments as well as forms and thus uses lots of beadwork and feathers. Her crochet technique is simple, mostly in single crochet. Photos, courtesy artist.

GRAINGER'S PASSION in cowhair, mohair, and beads. 13″ x 13″ x 11″.

Another view.

WINN'S WORRIES in cowhair, black lamé, feathers, and beads. All parts are movable for reassembly.

WINN'S WORRIES reassembled . . .

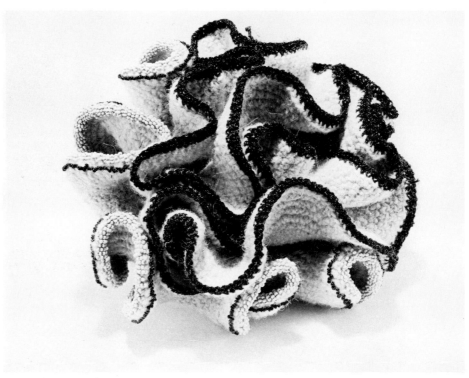

. . . and reassembled again . . .

. . . and still another way.

Boxes, Baskets, and Pottery

12

The potential of crochet as a type of soft pottery, for basketmaking, and as a vehicle for turning boxes into soft sculptures, is so vast that a whole book could be done elaborating on this chapter.

A pot is, of course, essentially a hat turned upside down. Consequently, the basic technique for making crochet pottery and baskets is that of making cupped rounds described in Chapter 6.

The method of making a crocheted pot is best likened to the coiling technique of the traditional potter. The pot is built row upon row of stitches, increasing for fullness, decreasing where the shape is to be narrowed down. By changing from heavy to thin yarns, thick to thin needles, the pot's wall and rim can be controlled.

Though crochet pots are in the "soft" category the choice of yarn helps in producing firm, self-supporting structures. Jutes, twines, and rug yarns are preferable to stretchy knits. Stiffness can be added by crocheting light wire in with your yarn. Walls can also be made quite rigid by brushing the inside of the pot with a mixture of half white glue and half water. This dries clear and has little effect on the surface texture. Many crocheters object to anything but a "pure yarn" pot, but we feel that the glue stiffening method is appropriate for certain types of projects and materials.

The symmetry and wit in Renie Breskin Adams's pottery give ample proof to our belief that a carefully wrought crochet piece can rival traditional pottery in aesthetic satisfaction. Renie brings her overall knowledge of textile designs to her students at the University of Wisconsin, but for her own personal medium she has been concentrating exclusively upon crochet. She works with nonstretchy fibers and small hooks. She begins her pots by stranding a number of fibers together, eliminating some strands as she gets to the tops of her pots, switching to smaller and smaller hooks.

A group of open pots. Notice the fine rims. These are achieved through the artist's technique of starting with 10 fat threads of yarns and finishing at the top with two thin strands. She also switches to correspondingly smaller hooks.

Speckled coffeepot, complete with spout, handle, and lid. To make the wall come straight up perpendicularly from the base, slip stitches were made around the last row in the base that formed loops on the surface, making a right angle in the fabric.

View of the inside of the coffeepot and the lid.

A POT OF STEW with beef, carrots, and potatoes all appropriately colored. This is done on a very small scale, measuring 2½″ tall and 3¾″ in diameter.

Plates of artificial food tend to be corny, but in this interpretation Renie Breskin Adams's plate of bacon with eggs and a blueberry muffin (essentially a closed pot) is so gracefully proportioned and subtly colored that it defies being stereotyped.

The cup and saucer surface is embroidered with a weaving stitch run over and under the ridges of the crochet stitch.

Still life in gray cotton. The light source of this one-piece form is created with stitchery on the crocheted forms.

One of a whole series of potted plants.

Deep rusts and greens make these look almost like real cactus plants. These are actually closed, stuffed pots, designed to be used as table pillows.

Crochet Pots as Plant Holders

With the increasing popularity of plants, one can't ever have too many plant holders. You can use a pot as a mold and work around it in double crochets and filet patterns. The covered box illustrated in the demonstration for working in the round over hard objects (p. 85) could easily be converted into a planter with the addition of straps. Raffia and twine are especially attractive for this purpose.

Even more unusual designs can be made by thinking of your planter as the flower itself. For example, a base pot can be built to resemble a chrysanthemum by adding separate little petals of individual shell stitches to the surface and adding a stem with leaves. Separate triangles can be used for flowers with more pointy leaves. Carrots, turnips, and other vegetable forms can be worked out as planters for vegetable plants. Always put a plastic disk of some sort into the bottom of your planter so that the plant can be watered without removing from the plant hanger. Margarine tops or coffee-can tops are excellent.

Chrysanthemum pot. The base is natural jute. Shell petals are worked separately in hot pink weaving wool and velour. Each shell is made by crocheting five single crochet stitches onto the base and then returning with one single into the first stitch, two half doubles into the second, three doubles into the third, two half doubles into the fourth, and a single into the last. Two more rows of single crochets, one in wool and one in velour, are worked on top of the second row. For the stem a folded floral wire is pushed through the bottom of the pot and wrapped with tape. For a fat stem, cotton can be worked underneath the tape. Single crochets in green wool are picked up around the bottom of the pot and worked all around the stem in a tube. The leaves are triangles crocheted off the stem.

Close-up of the chrysanthemum leaf, showing contrast of velour against wool. (See color section.)

This daisy-shaped pot started with the center of the daisy worked in a round increased to 60 stitches. Six leaves were worked separately onto the bottom, ten stitches each. After ten rows, each leaf was decreased as if making a triangle. The leaves were connected at the straight edges with single crochets worked along the outside. The raised ridge effect was repeated with an extra row of singles around the bottom and the pointy part of each leaf. The nylon planter was stiffened by brushing the inside with a mixture of half glue and half water.

Basket Sculptures

Basket sculpture. Mary Lou Higgins. Photo by Edward Higgins.

A basket can be much more than just that, as is strikingly illustrated with Mary Lou Higgins's TORSO BASKET of wool and acrilan. Photo by Edward Higgins.

Jean Williams Cacicedo has created an entire basketry series inspired by her love of nature and a real talent for translating her fantasies into sculptures alive with color, design, and imagery.

DESERT BASKET, rich in surface embellishments, resting firmly on tubular legs. 18″ x 16″ x 14″. Photo courtesy artist.

Detail of DESERT BASKET.

DESERT BASKET top.

FOREST BASKET with stuffed and appliquéd trees and leaves, sparked with tiny red berries. 16″ x 16″ x 18″.

MONA BIRD. Note the finely detailed beak.

Boxes

There's something about boxes that evokes an imaginative response in both amateur and professional artist. For the crocheter, an ordinary cigar box can become the basis for a soft sculpture. The idea of turning what is basically a discard into something useful and attractive has special appeal in this age of ecological awareness.

The following photos show how a cigar box was turned into a big floppy turtle and into an abstract female form. In both instances, the box was transformed without losing its functional value. These are merely two variations on a theme without end. Your box could be transformed into a house, a landscape, other animals, a giant plant, in short, whatever your fancy dictates.

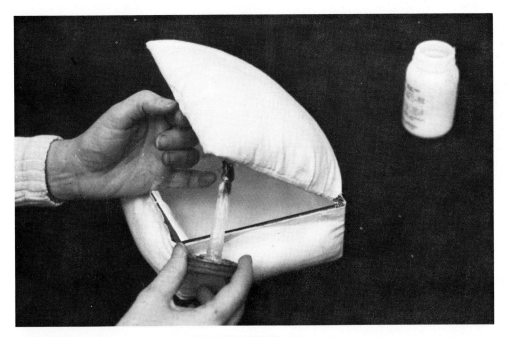

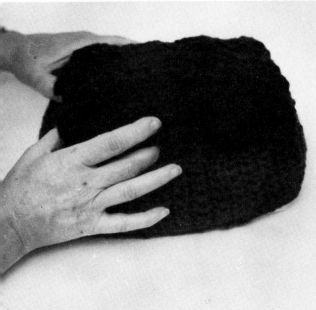

The top and sides of the box are covered with polyester fill and muslin. The muslin is glued in place with thick white glue such as Velverette. A staple gun could also be used.

The bottom of the box is covered with felt to which a strip of double crochets, long enough to fit all around the side of the box, is sewn. The top of the box is also covered. Shell stitches were used to symbolize a turtle's shell. The top piece must be stitched carefully to avoid jamming up the closing mechanism of the box.

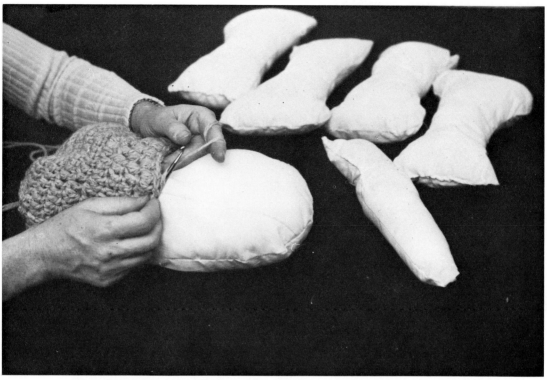

The turtle's feet, tail, and head are cut out in a muslin pattern and stuffed. These patterns are then covered in crochet, worked all around each piece in a tube.

Patterns are made to be attached to the central portion of the shell.

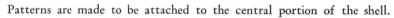

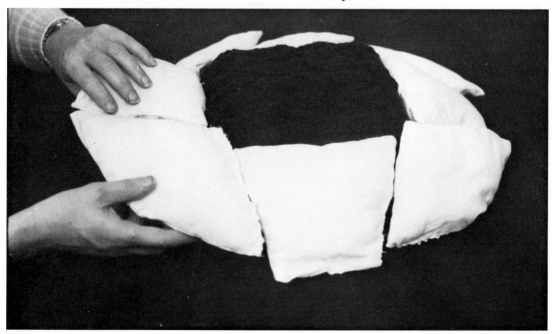

The finished turtle, in brown, beige, and maroon wool worsted. The maroon and beige are stranded together for the tweedy areas. The loop stitches around the shell add to the floppy effect. The eyes are appliquéd to the head.

The turtle shell can be lifted to make use of the very useful interior. It measures 26" in diameter and would make a fine trinket box-pillow.

An odd-lot purchase of old, not-too-clean chenille made us think of an old-time "Oomph Girl" down on her luck. The cigar box idea seemed a perfect one for bringing this to life. The head of pink corde is stuffed and sewn to the padded box top. The brown curls are made by making chains and working back along them with lots of increases. More chenille was crocheted around the padded bottom.

The head becomes a handle for opening and closing the box.

Norma Minkowitz also likes boxes and uses them to good advantage to make her pithy comments on the human condition. Here a velvet-covered box is filled with 2″ crocheted figures. The cotton and silky threads add an ethereal quality to THE SAMENESS OF US ALL. Photo by Kobler/Dyer Studio.

BRIDAL BOX. Knit, crochet, padding, and plastic tubing. 18″ x 14″. This was one of the featured pieces in the Baroque '74 show at the Museum of Contemporary Crafts. Photo by Kobler/Dyer Studio.

Another box worth studying for its meaning as well as its beauty and craftsmanship. HEAD BOX combines knit, crochet, trapunto, and padding. 13″ x 14″. Photo by Kobler/ Dyer Studios.

Big Boxes

Some time ago we received a brochure from a manufacturer of wooden boxes made for painting and decoupage ornamentation. When we saw a large hassock in the brochure, it seemed clear that crochet could work as well as if not better than painting or decoupage. It was decided to cover the box with a crocheted landscape.

A circle of heavy-duty felt was cut to fit the bottom of the hassock and hole-punched like leather. Crochet stitches were worked off the holes and the base was crocheted in the round. Various shades of green were yarned together for the grass, and the blue sky was interlaced with white clouds worked in an irregular tapestry pattern. It was later decided to give more dimension to the clouds, and fluffy cloudlike mohair was crocheted around the clouds, using loop stitches.

Houses were crocheted separately, with stitchery used for windows and doors. The three-dimensional sides were made by picking up the crossbars instead of the top loops for a sharply turned building side that could more easily be stuffed.

Trees and little people were also made separately. The tree branches are worked off the main part of the tree like scallops, but at random. The leaves are little picots worked in mohair and bouclé.

The figures were made by gluing ink-drawn stone heads to plasteline bodies. We used this non-hardening material because we wanted the figures to remain soft. The plasteline was coated with glue and water to keep it from cracking. The costumes are crocheted.

Crochet was worked all around, from a felt bottom. Various shades of green were yarned together for the grass bottom, and the blue sky was interlaced with white clouds. It was later decided to give a 3-D look to the cloud by loop stitching white mohair over the white areas of the base.

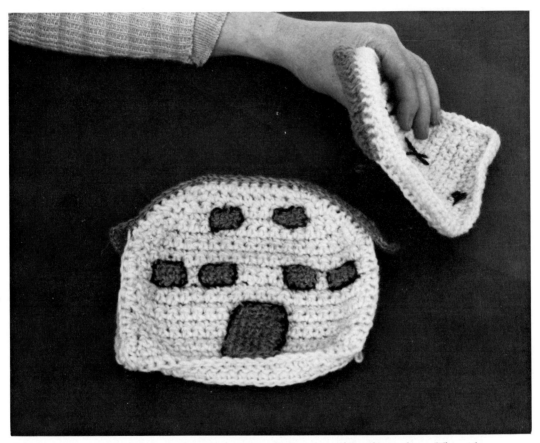

Houses were crocheted separately and later stuffed and appliquéd in place. The sides were turned at a sharp angle by picking up the crossbars instead of the top loops for the turning row.

Trees and people were also made separately. The branches are worked off the main trunk like scallops, but irregularly. The leaves are little picots in bouclé yarn. The figures were made with India-ink-drawn stone heads glued to plasteline bodies. The plasteline was protected against cracking with several coats of glue mixed with water. Crochet costumes were added last.

The lid of the hassock was made like a pillow. The design grew from the central sun shape, a circle with triangles. The features are crochet chains stitched to the surface. At the edge of the seat, decreases were made for a snug fit. No padding was needed since the hassock came with a padded top (see supply sources).

Overall view of the hassock. The inside was stained in dark brown.

Another view of the hassock.

Off the Beaten Path: a Final Look at a Miscellany of Creative Crochet

13

It's hard to end a book like this because there is no end to the unusual and exciting things being done with crochet by creative people everywhere. This book can only present the past and the present. The future chapters are still being written, or shall we say, crocheted.

And so we'd like to conclude with a roundup of a miscellany of creative crochet. Some of the pieces represent still another view of work by artists met earlier in the book; some are first-time meetings with artists whose work we felt would show up best in this special chapter.

Helen Bitar uses an innovative weaving technique for the central section of a wall-hanging blanket. Strips of crochet are woven in and out, attached by sewing at the back. Photo courtesy Boise Gallery of Art. (See color section.)

Norma Minkowitz also weaves strips of fabric together. Her woven strips are knitted, with small crocheted figures sewn to the top. AROUND AND AROUND, 10″ x 16″. Photo by Kobler/Dyer Studios.

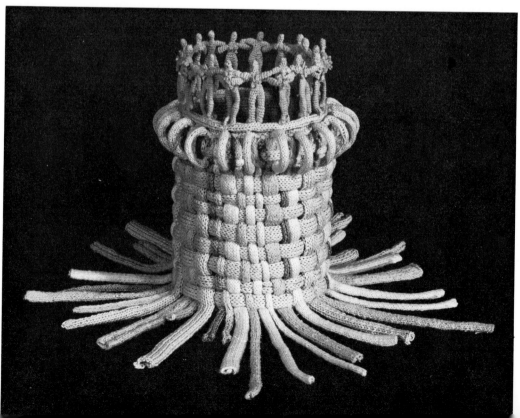

Crocheted and embroidered lamp covers were popular worktable projects during the nineteenth century. Mary Lou Higgins has given the basic idea more than a few new twists in the shape and materials used. Photo by Edward Higgins.

Lamp cover crocheted into the shape of a horse's head. Notice the way beads and feathers are brought into play to carry out the artist's imagery. Photo by Edward Higgins.

Another crocheted lamp cover, this time with the addition of fur as well as beads and feathers. Photo by Edward Higgins.

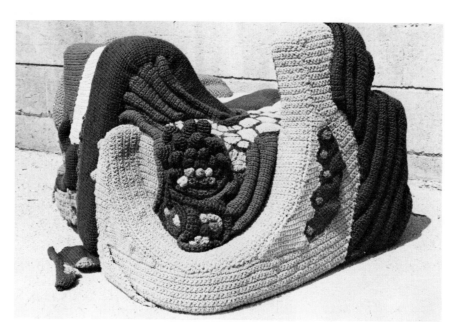

Shirley Saito crochets chairs, with foam pad armatures.

Crocheted sofa. Shirley Saito.

Crocheted chair. Shirley Saito.

Crocheted rug wool stretched over a rectangular mirror and embellished with curled crochet dangles made by working back along a base chain with lots of increases. Jane Knight. Photo by Richard Knight.

Three in a series of floor sculptures Sylvia Bushell calls CRATERS. The crochet is worked over wooden bases.

Dell Pitt Feldman used a table-height quintych as a backdrop for a fascinating family group. Mohair, lamé, and other yarns are used to "paint" in the details. Photo by Malcolm Varom.

Ron Goodman uses crochet to build forms of breathtaking fluidity. TO PRACTICE, RE-MEMBER TO PRACTICE TO REMEMBER is crocheted in orange wool. 11′ x 7′ x 5′. (See color section.) Photo courtesy artist.

TUBES IN CUBES OF ISOLATION. Ron Goodman. 10' x 15' x 6'. Photo courtesy artist.

This multifibered wall hanging by Bonnie Meltzer is the result of this transplanted Easterner's growing appreciation of the rain's effects upon the lush landscape of Oregon. RAIN DREAM measures 40″ x 50″. (See color section.)

It takes the artist's eye to see the symmetry in shapes often seen only in context of the ordinary and mundane. The forms are stuffed, crocheted in rug wool and stand 10 feet high. Jane Knight. Photo by Richard Knight.

CROCHET WITH A PICTURE ON THE WALL is a miniature environmental sculpture. Everything is in one piece. The picture on the wall is stitched and the overall dimensions are just 5" x 3" x 2¾". Renie Breskin Adams. (See color section.)

Jean Williams Cacicedo works primarily in crochet but makes use of her knowledge of appliqué. Here crochet and stuffed appliqué are combined in a mouth-watering potpourri of flowers and shapes. CALIFORNIA GARDEN. 24″ x 43″. Photo courtesy artist.

The possibilities for realizing fantasies with crochet are illustrated in Cinde Picchi's colorful SEA BEAST. Photo courtesy artist, from the Fairtree Gallery collection.

Margaret Ballantyne displays her fascination with embellishments as well as form in this abstract form crocheted with cowhair and lamé, trimmed with feathers and beads. Photo courtesy artist.

Another abstract fantasy by Margaret Ballantyne. Cowhair, silk cord, gold lamé, and feathers are used. Photo courtesy artist.

Finding just the right title for one's work is no mean accomplishment. Norma Minkowitz has a knack for aptly naming her splendidly crafted and unique knit and crochet commentaries. IF I WERE HATCHED. Photo by Kobler/Dyer Studios.

Another splendid example of mixed media and clever name calling, Mary Lou Higgins's combination of basketry and crochet sculpture. BASKETFUL OF DREAMS stands 2½ feet tall. Photo by Edward Higgins.

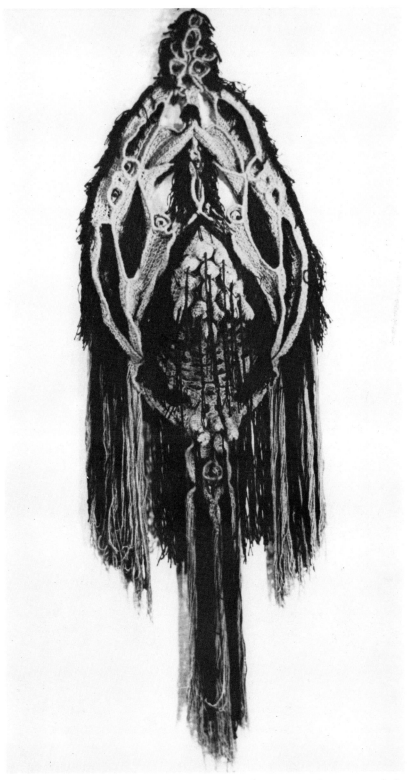

WALL SHRINE. Sculptural hanging by Walter Nottingham, one of the innovators in crochet as an art form.

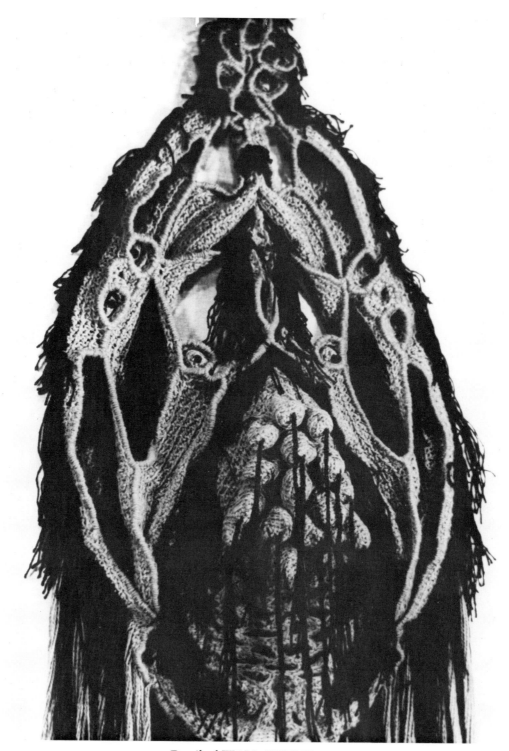

Detail of WALL SHRINE.

A spectacular modern-day phoenix by Sharon Hedges probably sums up better than anything just how far crochet can take you. The bird started as a cape and grew and grew and grew—to its present 9-foot magnificence. Sharon worked on the bird for 5 months. It's crocheted onto a hand-welded armature, stuffed with muslin-covered dacron. The underside is hand-quilted. Eighteen pounds of wool are used. The bird is constructed so that the head can be removed to allow for transportation.

We first saw the bird when it was still only partly complete. Even unfinished, it was an overwhelming spectacle. We next photographed it in Sharon's apartment and finally had the pleasure of seeing it hung to its best advantage, suspended over the balcony of the Museum of Contemporary Crafts.

Crocheted, stuffed, and quilted bird over welded steel armature. Sharon Hedges.

Close-up of the bird's head.

The head unsnaps to reveal the welded and stuffed interior.

The head can be completely removed to make the bird more easily transportable.

To give you an idea of the bird's perspective, a friend of Sharon's poses in front of it, at the same time affording us a rear view of Arlene Stimmel's handsome mirrored vest shown in Chapter 8.

Appendix

American-British Stitch Equivalency Chart

American	British
single crochet	double crochet
double crochet	treble crochet
half-double crochet	half treble crochet
treble crochet	double treble crochet

Crochet Hook Size Chart

*Steel	Aluminum	**Plastic	
1			
0	C		
00	D	D	3
	E	E	4
	F	F	5

G	G	6
H	H	8
I	I	9
J	J	10
K	K	10½
	Q (giant size)	
	S (giant size)	

Crochet Pattern Terminology and Symbols

asterisks	* Used to indicate beginning and end of repeat instructions
begin	beg
block	bl
chain	ch
chain stitch	ch st
decrease	dec
double crochet	d c
half-double crochet	half dc or h dc
increase	inc
over	o
picot	p
previous row	pr
row	r
round	rnd
single crochet	sc or s cr
skip	sk
slip stitch	sl st
stitches	sts
together	tog
treble crochet	tr c
wrap around hook	wrh (same as yarn over or over)
yarn over	y o (see over)

* Steel hooks are made in additional sizes from 14 on downward, but these are not listed individually since modern crocheters rarely use hooks this fine.
** Plastic hooks come in letter and number sizes.

Yarn Information Chart

Type of Yarn	Description
Wool worsted	Soft, smooth, widely available in many colors. Allow for stretchiness.
Wool rug yarns	Strong, nonstretchy, coarse in texture.
Wool rya rug yarn	Qualities of other wool rug yarns with more give or stretch factor.
Scottish and Swedish wools	Soft, thin, stretchy; available in subtle color hues.
Irish and fishermen's yarns	Medium thick and heavy types available, contains natural oils; natural and earth colors.
Wool cowhair	Very coarse but strong, with some give. Good for hangings more than wearables.
Wool novelties	Alpaca, mohair bouclé, and other fuzzy wools. Hard to see stitches and to rip. Good for accents, dressy clothes.
Cotton	Thin threads to Speed Crosheen, smooth, colorful, nonstretchy.
Cotton string	Strong, various thicknesses; some colors, though natural and black usually only colors carried in stores.
Rayon novelties	Includes corde, which is rayon wrapped around cotton, shiny ribbons, soutache. Corde and soutache work up very well but should not be used for anything that will get heavy use; ribbon is slippery to crochet but ideal for shiny accents.
Miscellaneous novelties	Chenille—soft, velvetlike material; expensive but can be used for accents. Metallics—stiff and thin. Best for jewelry, encasing hard objects, accents.
Cotton-rayon mixtures	Cotton rayon rug yarns are stretchier than wool rug yarn. Stitches show clearly. Good, inexpensive for beginners.
Linen	Available in fine through coarse range. Coarse linens in natural only. Very firm, nonstretchy and strong. Expensive.
Nylons, Orlons, and acrylics	Nylons and Orlons are soft and stretchy, the synthetic equivalent to wool worsteds. Acrylic rug yarns are strong, easy to crochet. Synthetic colors tend to be harder than natural yarns. Acrylics, unlike wool, will not deteriorate if exposed to outdoor elements.

Bibliography

Blackwell, Liz. *A Treasury of Crochet Patterns*. New York: Charles Scribner's Sons, 1971.

Caulfield, Sophie Frances Anne and Saward, Blanche C. *The Dictionary of Needlework*. Originally published in 1882. Facsimile editions: Arno Press and Dover Publications, 1972.

Dawson, Mary M. *A Complete Guide to Crochet Stitches*. New York: Crown Publishers, 1972.

De Dillemont, Therese. *Encyclopedia of Needlework*. Milhouse, France, DMC Library.

Edson, Nicki Hitz, and Stimmel, Arlene. *Creative Crochet*. New York: Watson-Guptill, 1973.

Feldman, Del Pitt. *The Crocheter's Art*. New York: Doubleday, 1974.

Harrison, E. *The Young Ladies' Journal—Complete Guide to the Work Table*. London: Merton House, 1884.

Kiewe, Heinz Edgar. *The Sacred History of Knitting*. Oxford, England: Art Needlework Industries Ltd., 1967.

266

Lindsey, Ben. *Irish Lace: Its Origin and History*. Dublin: Hodges, Figgis & Co., 1886.

MacKenzie, Clinton D. *New Design in Crochet*. New York: Van Nostrand Reinhold Company, 1972.

Mon Tricot. *Knitting Dictionary*. New York: Crown Publishers, 1972.

Stephens, Mrs. Ann S. *The Ladies' Complete Guilde to Crochet, Fancy Knitting and Needlework*. New York: Garret & Co., 1854.

Techy, Margaret. *Filet Crochet Lace: How to Make It*. New York and London: Harper & Bro., 1943.

Thomas, Mary. *Mary Thomas's Knitting Book*. New York: Dover Publications, 1972.

Whitney, Le Jeune. *Crocheting with Swistraw*. Privately printed. California: 1972.

Publications

CRAFTS HORIZON
44 West 53 St.
New York, N.Y. 10019
Bimonthly

CREATIVE CRAFTS
Drawer 700
Newton, N.J. 06869

SHUTTLE SPINDLE & DYEPOT
Handweavers Guild of America
998 Farmington Avenue
West Hartford, Conn. 06107

WESTART
Box 1396
Auburn, Calif. 94546

THE WORKING CRAFTSMAN
Box 42 B
Northbrook, Ill. 60062

Sources of Supplies

Crochet hooks and yarns are readily available whether you live in a rural village or a big city. Variety stores, department stores, even supermarkets and drugstores, feature yarn displays. Small shops specializing in knitting and crochet materials can be found in many neighborhoods. Hardware stores carry interesting assortments of string, twine, and rope.

Use your classified directory to build up your own supply resource list. In addition to listings for yarns, check those for MARINE SUPPLIES, WEAVERS' SUPPLIES, CORDAGE SUPPLIES, LEATHER, BEADS. The out-of-the-way places you can visit yourself are the most fun. Here in New York, we like to browse around Canal Street and the Lower East Side for novelty cords and string, scrap leather and junk items to be used like beads. A bit further uptown in the East Village there is Studio Del, while across town in the West Village lots of fine yarns can be found at Threadbare Unlimited. We'd love to spend months just combing through every city for its own offbeat little shops, but even if time permitted, a listing of such addresses would serve little purpose for readers who are scattered throughout the world. Instead, we have compiled a list of suppliers who will fill mail orders. This list is by no means complete and thus not to be interpreted as our own exclusive endorsement. We suggest that readers refer to the ads in some of the magazines listed at the end of the bibliography as an ongoing source of supplies.

Yarns

Berga/Ullman
Box 831 L
Westerly Road
Ossining, N.Y. 10562
Swedish wool. Samples $3. Superprompt
    shipments.

Dick Blick
Box 1268
Galesburg, Ill. 61401
Ask for their special catalogue for weaving and related crafts.

Christopher Farm Wool Yarn
RFD 2
Richmond, Maine 04357
They raise sheep here. Lovely handspuns.
    Samples 50¢.

William Condon & Sons
65 Queen St.
Charlottetown, P.E.I., Canada

Contessa Yarns
Box 37
Lebanon, Conn. 06249
Novelty yarns, silks, wools for weavers.
    Announcements of new yarn arrivals
    sent to those on mailing list. Samples 25¢.

Coulter Studios
118 East 59 St.
New York, N.Y. 10022
Imported and domestic yarns, wooden crochet hooks.

Countryside Handweavers
Box 1225
Mission, Kans. 66222

Crafts Yarns of Rhode Island
Box 385
Pawtucket, R.I. 02862
Yarns, cords, novelties. Samples 50¢.

CUM
5 Rosemersgrade
1362
Copenhagen, K., Denmark
Lovely Danish yarn and linens. Does not
    sell directly but will send information
    about distributor and huge sample book
    for $3. (See School Arts Products.)

Dharma Trading Co.
Box 1288
Berkeley, Calif. 94701
Yarns, cords, dyes. Samples 50¢.

Eskimo Yarn Co.
81 Essex St.
New York, N.Y. 10002
50¢ for sample card of basic yarn assortment.

Frederick Fawcett, Inc.
129 South St.
Boston, Mass. 02111
Specializes in linens. Sample, $1.

Fiber Studio
P.O. Box 356
Sudbury, Mass. 01776
All weight wool rug yarn, novelty weaving yarns, wool/Dacron blends.

Folklorico
Box 625
Palo Alto, Calif.
Mexican handspuns. Samples 75¢.

Fort Crailo Yarns Co.
2 Green St.
Rensselaer, N.Y. 12144
Wools, cottons. Large assortment.

Greentree Ranch Wools
163 N. Carter Lake Road
Loveland, Colo. 80537
Goat hair, Cum, and other imported fine yarns, raw fleece for spinning and dyes. Catalogue 25¢.

Home Yarns
1849 Coney Island Avenue
Brooklyn, N.Y. 11230
Novelty yarns. Samples 35¢.

Lily Mills
Shelby, N.C. 28150
$1 catalogue; att: Weaving Department.

Ma Goodness
1614 Farrlon Rd.
Millville, N.J. 08332
$2 for price list and samples of lovely handspuns; many thick yarns.

The Mannings
East Berlin, Pa. 17316
All types yarns, cords. Catalogue 50¢.

Mexiskeins
Box 1624
Missoula, Mont. 59801
Thick Mexican handspuns, rich colors. Samples $1.

Naturalcraft
2199 Bancroft Way
Berkeley, Calif. 94704
Yarns, beads, feathers, books. Catalogue 75¢.

Potomac Yarns
P. O. Box 2368.
Chapel Hill, N.C. 27514
Free samples of rug yarns; mostly acrylic, some nylon and wool. Some good earth colors. Inexpensive. Fast shipments.

School Arts Products Co., Inc.
1201 Broadway
New York, N.Y. 10001
Wide assortment wool, cottons; miscellaneous supplies like swifts and yarn winders. Distributor for CUM yarns.

Shelburne Spinners
Box 651
Burlington, Vt. 05401
25¢ brochure and samples.

Some Place
2991 Adeline St.
Berkeley, Calif. 94703

Straw Into Gold
P. O. Box 2904
Oakland, Calif. 94618
Yarns, beads, books; very readable. Catalogue 75¢.

Tahki Imports Ltd.
336 West End Ave.
New York, N.Y. 10023
Greek, Irish, and Colombian handspuns. Free catalogue.

The Unique
211 East Bijou
Colorado Springs, Colo. 80902
Imported yarns. Sample card $1.

Yarn Center
866 Sixth Avenue
New York, N.Y. 10001
Wool, synthetics. Will make up sample cards if you specify type and brand yarn and send 35¢. Flyers on specials.

Yarn Depot
545 Sutter St.
San Francisco, Calif. 94102
Assortment of yarns, beads. Inquire about bimonthly sample club.

Beads

Bead Game
505 N. Fairfax Ave.
Los Angeles, Calif. 90036
Beads, mirrors, leather, and suede. Catalogue 50¢.

Gloria's Glass Garden
Box 1990
Beverly Hills, Calif. 90213

Jewelart
7753 Densmore Avenue
Van Nuys, Calif. 90027

Sheru
49 West 38 St.
New York, N.Y. 10018

Walbead
38 West 37 St.
New York, N.Y. 10018

Leather

Sax Arts and Crafts
207 North Milwaukee
Milwaukee, Wis. 53202

Tandy Crafts
See local classified directory

Lee Ward
840 North State
Elgin, Ill. 60120

Unfinished Wooden Hassocks

Bentwood Products Co.
P.O. Box 615
Fort Valley, Ga. 31030

Miscellaneous

Louise McCrady
30 Rockwell Place
West Hartford, Conn. 06107
Shirret needle and auxiliary supplies.

Some Place
2991 Adeline St.
Berkeley, Calif. 94703
Hand-carved crochet hooks.

Index